Lonely as a Goldfish

Also by this author:

The God of the Low Places:
Finding God in Depression

Lonely as a Goldfish

A Manual on Combating Loneliness for Senior Citizens

Karen Mo

Cover illustration by Mickey Moscynski; cover design by Matthew Brownstein

ISBN

Dedication

To Susan and Matthew Brownstein, Mickey and Marianne Moscynski, Thomas and Beth Moscynski.
Thanks, kids.

lpm

Table of Contents

Preface and acknowledgements

I was sitting with a discussion group of seven senior citizens who were asked to name the biggest problem they are facing right now. One mentioned friction with her adult kids, another financial problems. The next said, "Loneliness," and sat back in her chair. The remaining three agreed with her. "Oh, yes, loneliness."

Although I too had problems with loneliness, I was astounded by the overwhelming response. How could four people sitting next to each other all feel lonely? It would seem that lonely people would attract each other and no longer be lonely, clicking together like the little buttons on the bottom of refrigerator magnets. Yet we each have our reserve. We are islands. Fortunately the situation is not hopeless. With a little encouragement we can build a bridge.

This book analyzes loneliness: what it is, how it feels, what it does to us, and what we can do about it. As with the discussion group, it is one of the most pervasive topics of our time.

We moved in separate spheres before COVID-19 and the lockdown. If we already had some contacts, we were buffered from the full impact. Yet as the restrictions ease, we still need to reach out to others to avoid being in the same isolated rut.

We can overcome it with simple changes in how we connect with each other. Some of the members of the discussion group exchanged phone or text numbers. We became accustomed to contacting each other at discrete intervals, and friendships developed. My life has been embellished as a result.

I'm here writing to you, and you're reading what I have written. Already we are not alone. All we need to do is to connect through whatever medium.

At times we don't feel a need to connect. We are content within ourselves, perhaps playing music or reading or making bead jewelry or merely musing. In a genuine period of solitude, we feel fulfilled, not alone.

At other times we feel a need to be in touch with someone, either in person or through some other means of communication. If we find nobody, we experience loneliness, a painful condition. We can respond by expanding our circle of possible connections, by reaching out to even the most fleeting of experiences.

This book proposes to enable you to do both: to be comfortable within solitude and to expand your circle of connections. The net result will be less lonely and more complete time. I hope to amuse you along the way.

Special thanks to the Chevy Chase Writing Group who faithfully read over each chapter of the work in progress: Jane Hancock (leader, God rest her soul), Mary Simeone, Christine Alexanians, Barbara Lewis, and Mina Kirby. Thanks also to Halbert Thomas who offered much insight. I acknowledge with gratitude the support of Stepping Stones (especially Veronica Gardner-Mendoza) and Sparr Heights Senior Center.

List of Contributors

The following have contributed their experiences in the indicated chapters. Many thanks to them for sharing.

NAME	CHAPTER
Connie Stuebing	2. The Cold
Elizabeth Whisnant	4. Self-Esteem
Elizabeth Whisnant	5. Solitude
Halbert Thomas	6. Meditation and Mindfulness
Mary Simeone	9. Volunteer Positions
Deven Ronnquist	11. Independent Living
Patricia Cowden	15. Being Sick and Alone
Alethea	18. Friendship

1. Lonely People

A writer out of loneliness is trying to communicate like a distant star sending signals. He isn't telling, or teaching, or ordering. Rather, he seeks to establish a relationship with meaning, of feeling, of observing.
John Steinbeck

Fifty years ago. I spent the evening at the apartment of Tony, a friend of some friends, discussing the state of the world with the earnestness of college freshmen at The University of Michigan. With Motown playing in the background, we discussed our respective philosophies of life, reasons for being, goals. It was the turbulent sixties. If you are a Baby Boomer, the following are familiar:

- o The Vietnam War was ramping up. Every week more troops were sent over, and every week more soldiers were coming home in body bags, some we knew. We had friends living in Canada to avoid the draft.
- o Conventional politics were ceding power. Lyndon Johnson said that if nominated, he would not run; if elected he, would not serve. I heard the speech in Wisconsin where I was campaigning for Eugene McCarthy.
- o The Black Action Movement led student strikes on campus. Their goals were simple, 10% minority enrollment, but the university

didn't know how or where to recruit, how to prepare people who had not had access to college prep courses, how to fund lower income students. Tony was deeply aware that the black person was still a different kind of person with different prospects.

o Disturbances on campus were common. It was not unheard of to round a corner and see twenty protesters of an unnamed issue skirmishing with as many police. Kent State was on the horizon.

o With the increased prescription of "the pill" to single women, the sexual revolution was in full swing. The dorms relaxed their curfews and visitation policies. Everybody, male and female alike, was on the hunt.

o Women poked at the glass ceiling, but it didn't crack. They began wearing pantsuits to work instead of shirtwaists. Dorms dropped the requirement to wear skirts to the evening meal, and students wore jeans to classes. With the insertion of a triangular piece of fabric, they became bell bottoms.

o Even the venerable Catholic Church convened Vatican II for review of deep-held traditions. Rules on fasting and abstinence were relaxed (no more meatless Fridays except during Lent), and the Mass was said in the vernacular instead of Latin. Women no longer had to cover their heads.

At the end of the evening, as we walked across the campus to my dorm, Tony made the comment, "Some people are lonely, but you, girl – you're lonesome." Every once in a while someone will make a comment that is

so heavy with truth that it hits home like a weight travers-
ing to the bottom of one's stomach. Thud. I don't know
why he said it, and he didn't extrapolate. I knew that his
diagnosis was accurate; by nature I was a lonesome person.

A distancing world. From the late sixties to today,
from our point of embarking on a life to completing our
profession in it, the world around us has transformed and
yet stayed the same.

In the morning the alarm beeps instead of buzzes,
shows the time in square blue numerals instead of a
round clock face. Gone is the Corningware coffeepot that
sat on the back burner of the stove, replaced by a drip
coffee maker. If you set it up the night before, you can
tell your smart-home device to start the coffee, and the
coffee maker will spring into action.

If you prefer, you can use an even newer Keurig
single-cup coffee maker. I drink instant coffee with water
heated in the microwave, also an appliance that wasn't
around when we were starting out.

Grocery stores are twice the size and carry ten
kinds of milk. Cash registers used to be mechanical devices, and clerks counted out the change in the palm of
your hand. "Two pennies make 65¢, a dime makes 75¢,
and a quarter makes a dollar." Now computerized cash
registers show the total change due. The clerk puts everything in your hand at once, coins and bills and the receipt
besides, and you are left trying to sort it and count it
while the next customer's purchases are already sliding
down the counter. As often as not, I just jam it all in my
pocket to deal with later. The smallest of small distractions, it adds to our feelings of being automated away.

Geopolitics have changed and yet not changed.
The Soviet Union has returned to being Russia. Korea

was the war of the fifties, and today North Korea is a nuclear threat. Meanwhile we go on fighting without end a war against terrorism in the Middle East.

People from cooperating nations live in the International Space Station circling the globe for months at a time. Choked with carbon emissions, our atmosphere is warming and our seas are rising. The world our grandchildren inherit may again be very different.

Every home has a computer, a screen and a mouse with which we have a love-hate relationship. It brings us instant news and immediate friends if we can find the right icon. Some homes have smart devices which listen to our every word and doorbell cams which scrutinize our neighborhood.

It's not that we long for the old civilization, but we have the feeling that the modern era is sliding past us as we watch helpless to engage in it. We feel distanced from out grandkids who know how to deal with every Minecraft monster, while we can't build a decent structure. When I recognized a torch on the screen, my grandson told me that I was not a total dweeb.

We experience being isolated and apart from the mainstream. People we never heard of are winning SAG awards.

The feeling of loneliness. Everybody experiences being alone at some point during the day or week. However for some persons with the character trait of being lonely, the lonely feeling goes beyond occasional moments of solitude. We have an unmet need, and it is painful.

Two out of five Americans report feeling lonely on a regular basis. It feels like physical pain; the same regions of the brain are activated by pain and by loneliness. It presents similar health risks as smoking or obesity.

On the other hand, face-to-face contact boosts production of endorphins, the brain chemicals that ease pain and enhance well-being.

Some of the feelings we experience during moments of loneliness include the following:

o *Emptiness.* We feel hollow inside, that something is missing. We have no joy to fill our souls, no peace to fill our being. We are lacking.

o *Longing.* When we recognize the emptiness, we feel a yearning to fill it in, to make ourselves whole. We may try to find solutions, something that will fill in the void. Mentally we search desperately, but nothing fits the piece in the puzzle. We may turn to addictions.

o *Ennui.* Despite the driving force of emptiness to try to fill in, we are immobilized. We can do nothing concrete. Nothing seems worth doing. We may consider an activity that might help pull ourselves out, but we don't pursue it. We stay in our chair or even our bed unable to get up the resolve to act. The drive of the feeling of emptiness and the immobility of the ennui create an internal conflict.

o *Lassitude.* We are like an eighteenth-century sailing ship becalmed at sea with no wind to fill its sails. We cannot move.

o *Boredom.* We are left unsure of what to do with ourselves. We are unable to pick up a pen to write or a phone to call somebody. We are especially bored with simple amusements like television. We cannot attach to anything to distract us. It is all the same.

o *Melancholy.* We feel the blues, sadness, or heaviness of heart. We are weighed down by our unresolved longing, a physical sensation that we cannot shake.

o *Anxiety*. We feel desperate to move, to get free of these feelings, and at the same time we are mired in muck, unable to take even the smallest step. The harder we try, the greater the sense of conflict becomes. We may even experience physical symptoms in head, stomach, or chest.

o *Fear*. The inescapability of the feelings makes us afraid. We cannot remain in this state indefinitely, and yet we have no hope of escaping it. Something has to give, and we are beginning to suspect that the something might be us, that we're headed toward a path of self-destruction.

That description of the feelings is brutal, but it has to be done. We need to be able to look the beast straight in the eye in order to be able to stare it down, to be motivated to reach beyond ourselves.

A goldfish in a bowl is lonely. On his shelf in the pet store, he can see other goldfish in other bowls, and all are lonely. On another shelf, he can see multiple fish swimming in square tanks, all interacting with each other, but none of them notice the goldfish. Sometimes this is how it feels to be older in America. We are each alone in our own spaces, without social connection, isolated. How can there be so many of us and yet each of us is all alone?

Gregariousness. Like many other species of animals, humans are gregarious. They learned early in their history that they hunted and gathered better in groups. At night they banded together for mutual protection, and they shared child-care responsibilities to make their efforts more productive. They learned to fashion tools out of the material at hand, and they learned that they could use certain sounds to convey a meaning. Human beings became interdependent.

They were referred to as tribes. Later words to indicate groups of humans have included a nomadic pack, a village, a city, an army, a fiefdom, a kingdom, a neighborhood, a work unit, a party, a meeting, a convention, a fan base, and a mob.

Groups of animals have their own names. We know that a group of lions is a pride, and a group of wolves is a pack. Elephants, cattle, goats, and sheep all travel in herds. According to science-basedlife.wordpress.com, we find the following names for groups of animals:

Animal	Group
porcupines	prickle
monkeys	barrel
hyenas	cackle
rhinoceroses	crush

Silence. A goldfish bowl is silent. The fish's fins make no noise, and the water buffers sounds from outside the bowl. If I live alone, with the occasional exception of the phone (usually a solicitor), nothing happens unless I make it happen. I can hear my neighbor's dog barking or the maintenance person cutting grass, but inside my apartment all is silent unless I turn on the radio. If I lay a book down on Tuesday, it will be there on Thursday unless I put it away on Wednesday.

In a skilled nursing facility, a lot of people are bustling about, and yet an individual experiences a lot of silence. According to the Institute on Aging, in the 17 years between 1992 and 2009, admissions to skilled nursing facilities increased almost threefold, from 28 to 80 per 1,000 Medicare beneficiaries. Up to one hundred or more goldfish bowls are in one facility.

The lack of stimulation is in itself mind-deadening. We experience the feelings of loneliness. What *should* we be doing now? What many of these feelings have in common is the sense that we are unable to do something to ease the loneliness. That is real, and yet it is part of a down spiral. Loneliness has a negative connotation, a sense of not being desired.

Other people. You can feel not connected even while among other people. Recall sixth grade, when there was an "in" group and a "fringe" group. Perhaps you were always in the fringe group, standing by the in group on the playground but never acknowledged, never spoken to directly, as they planned the upcoming sleepover at Jane's house. Never invited.

The adult equivalent is the cocktail party or the picnic or family reunion or whatever gathering to which a lot of people are invited. You scan the small conversational clusters, choose one with friendly faces to stand beside, but never become a member. And so with another cluster and another. Is it you or is it them?

You enjoy listening to the conversations, but you feel self-conscious. You know that you are not on the same playing field, that internally you feel broken, that you do not belong. You put up a good front to hide the brokenness.

And yet how do you know that they are not also putting on their party faces, that they are not carrying some degree of brokenness? Maybe broken is okay, even the norm. How do you know that you don't have something to give them? Your self-esteem is a problem.

Even in a one-on-one relationship you can feel misunderstood and lonely, an intimate relationship that has cooled or a friendship that has gone stale. The most important conversation of the week has been how to get rid of the dandelions.

This book is a manual for survival. We suggest changes that you can make to better experience feelings of loneliness. We explore solitude, loneliness, and togetherness, the existence of the times of each, and what each does for our being. We see that times of loneliness are inevitable, and we look at ways to deal with these.

We suggest changes to turn your times of loneliness into solitude, times of peace with being alone. Being alone does not necessarily mean feeling empty. Solitude can be filled with the satisfaction of things done alone whether small tasks or hobbies or meditating. We have a chapter on solitude later in the book.

We learn to reach out to others and increase our options for human contact. Friendships don't grow overnight. We experiment with exchanged pleasantries, grow bolder with polite conversations, evaluate, and eventually take the plunge into shared relationships. We also have a chapter on friendships and relationships later in the book.

Hopefully we learn to make our days more fulfilling by growing an increment at a time, a challenge at a time.

Challenge for Change: Smile. Whenever you think of it, smile to yourself. Let your lips turn up. You will feel better. Especially smile to other people when you encounter them, whether passing on a sidewalk or sitting down to dinner with them. Make it a habit to smile.

Even if you are wearing a mask, smile anyhow. Your whole face lights up.

2. The Cold

How cold is it?

It is so cold that the polar bears are buying polyester-filled jackets.

It is so cold we use bowls of soup for curling stones in the Olympics.

It is so cold we didn't clean the house – we just defrosted it.

Cold. Feeling cold and feeling lonely have much in common. Both feelings exist because you are without something. In the case of loneliness, you lack the comfort of human warmth. In extreme cases, cold is bleak, stark, and potentially fatal.

Extreme cold can be dangerous. Suppose you are walking along a wintry road on a subzero day, and you slip on an icy patch and tumble down a long hill into a ditch. The cold penetrates through to your bones. You know you cannot survive for long because you are at risk of frostbite or even hypothermia.

Looking up you see people passing by, but they do not look down to see you. You need outside help. You need to get someone's attention, to yell or wave so that they will look down and see your predicament.

Likewise with the psychological situation of extreme loneliness. You have tried to bootstrap yourself out, but have fallen back in failure. You are showing symptoms of depression, of not taking care of your basic needs, like food, rest, and exercise. You feel in need of professional help. Meanwhile the rest of the world goes by oblivious.

Sometimes it will be up to you to let the busy world know that you are falling behind. A simple statement, "I need help," can set the ball rolling with a trusted loved one, teacher, peer, primary care physician, or voice mail of a psychiatric clinic. Otherwise you are at risk of acting out until you receive attention.

Needing outside help is an extreme case. Most instances of loneliness are not that drastic. You have the option to make changes that would improve your comfort level.

Consider now **a cold room**, perhaps sixty degrees or less. Chilly and uncomfortable but not life-threatening, the room is more like the ordinary experience of loneliness. By putting on a sweater or a shawl, you can trap your own body warmth to feel more comfortable, similar to using self-help to decrease your feelings of loneliness. You learn to find a measure of contentment in solitude.

Solitude feels good. What solitude means is that you are alone in a time of peace, of feeling comfortable just in the presence of yourself. Without external chatter you may or may not include activities such as hobbies or reading or television or simply reflecting.

As you age you may find that you enjoy – even require – more times of solitude. You may have retired from fulltime endeavors. You have handed back the grandkids for the day. You are free to fill your hours as you wish. Although the air is still chilly in this room, solitude can be a good feeling. .

Warm air. Going further, you can defrost the house, warm up the air around you. Throw another log on the fireplace. Nudge up the thermostat a notch. You become warmer when you have social contacts around.

By making change you encourage friendships and relationships. The air can glow.

Moving through these three stages of cold—
loneliness, solitude, and social contact –you can achieve
some warmth in your life. How much depends on circumstances or on you. You can decide how much effort
you want to put into it and what comfort level you want
to reach.

Old age. The skin on my inner forearm is wrinkled
like a cabbage that has been sliced in half. How did that
happen? The transformation to physical old age has come
on slowly from the outset. From the first burp my body
has been programmed to move me through youth and
middle age to seniordom. Now I also fart.

Five areas of life can be defined as being affected:
physical, mental, emotional, social, and financial, but we
can make no generalizations for any one person. For each
category there are exceptions. Witness Gladys Burill who
at the age of 92 ran the 2012 Honolulu Marathon in
9:53:16, or Jonathan Mendes who at the age of 96 ran the
2016 New York City Marathon in 11:23.

Consider Chet Jaeger who at 92 leads and plays
cornet with the still-popular Night Blooming Jazzmen.

We are said to be more difficult emotionally, but
our power struggles with our kids over how to run our
lives are not one-sided. And we kind find numerous examples of senior citizens socializing on the beaches of
Nice.

Regardless we have all fallen into a category
known as "old age" and characterized by deficiencies.
Nobody agrees on when old age begins. According to
The Huffington Post (11/21/15), old age is defined as follows:

5-year-olds: Old age begins at 13.
13-year-olds: Old age begins at 30.
30-year-olds: Old age begins at 50.
50-year-olds: Old age begins at 75.
75-year-olds: Never. And go away.

One thing is clear: old age has no transition to yet another phase. Whether one is in old age for five years or thirty-five, the next phase is death. Different people carry that knowledge in various ways: denial, acceptance, avoidance.

Self-identification. We are who we are. I can picture the eleven-year-old girl sitting at a wooden desk in her bedroom determined to write a novel. After a few pages I abandoned the attempt for lack of a plot, and I didn't pick it up again until thirty years later, but I am that person, not a former person or a potential person. I am at a wooden desk typing into my computer.

When I was a child, I knew I fit the label, but I didn't think of myself as a child. My ways didn't seem childish to me. I was a person. I was Me. When I was in my forties I carried the label middle-aged, but I felt like Me. Now in my seventies, I still feel like Me.

Ceridwen Dovey wrote, "Most of what has been written in the sociological literature about life in our seventies, eighties, and nineties suggests that who we are when we are old remains pretty close to who we were when we were young."[1]

That is not to say we cannot change. We can make up our minds to adopt new patterns of living. We can become more outgoing, more open to friendships, less lonely. This book tells that story.

---

[1] Ceridwen Dovey, "what old age is really like," *The New Yorker*, Oct. 1, 2015.

Attitudes. How do others see people of old age in general? Often the perception of older generations is negative. We do not contribute to society. We suck up Social Security. We clog the health care system. We forget things and repeat ourselves.

As a result of a survey of attitudes toward aging, Thomas Hess wrote, "… negative attitudes about aging are pervasive in our culture and are reflected in affective, cognitive, and behavioral responses of individuals and groups of all ages. In addition, evidence shows that implicit attitudes may be even more strongly negative than explicit ones."[2]

As a group we feel ourselves no longer a member of the mainstream of society. That in itself generates a sense of alone.

The more association a person has with the elderly, and the age of the person who is associating, can result in fewer negative stereotypes. As individuals we can be accepted in specific relationships. Once people know us, they put aside the general expectations and accept us for who we are.

Bereavement. When someone who fills a special place in your heart is taken away, that place is empty, and it hurts. Like a cave that has opened in a rock face after an earthquake, you cannot make the cave go away, but in time you may grow accustomed to it and even transform the memories within to an okay place to be. Grief or bereavement is the state of loss when someone close has died. It is a significant form of loneliness.

[2] Thomas M. Hess, "Attitudes toward Aging and Their Effects in Behavior," *Handbook of the Psychology of Aging,* Academic Press, 2006.

People who are grieving experience crying spells, trouble sleeping, and change of appetite. They often react to the loss with feelings of depression, anger, and guilt. They may find that it is difficult to concentrate or that they are easily distracted.

If possible, draw on the support of friends and family. Let them know what you need—a hug, time together, time apart, talking about the loved one, talking about anything but, being included. They will say, "I'm sorry," and the moment will be difficult but necessary. Respond with a simple, "Thank you." Even if you break down, it is okay. Carry tissues. If you need to, excuse yourself briefly. They understand.

If family and friends are not available, find a community. Consider a move to assisted living. Find a bereavement group. Visit a small coffee shop every day at the same time. Get to know the waitpersons and the other regulars at least to nod to. Create a familiar environment. Experiment with communicating by cell phone and text.

Bring the experience into the fiber of your life, and decide how to move forward. Make a commitment to take care of yourself as much as possible, to sleep if you can and to watch your nutrition even if not hungry.

Above all be compassionate to yourself. Allow yourself the depths of emotions which you feel. Permit a smile if you remember a particularly tender moment of your lives together. Accept the finality of the loss. You will make a new life which continues to respect the memory of your loved one at the same time as allowing you to define new roles.

Depending on the belief system, some feel it is never too late to communicate strong feeling to the deceased. Many believe that we may still express them to the loved one who has moved on to another life. "So…if you've lost a loved one in a situation where there was still something unresolved, where there was still a tension that needed easing, where you should have been more attentive, or where you feel badly because you never adequately expressed the affirmation and affection that you might have, know it's not too late. It can still be done!" [Father Ronald Rolheiser OMI, "Unfinished Relationships," *Angelus*, March 15, 2019].

The grieving process takes time, maybe six months or two years or longer. The initial pain should start to subside as you proceed along the path toward reintegration with your life. If that doesn't happen, if you appear inconsolable and stuck in your grieving, it might be what is called "complicated grief." Often professional help from a therapist can enable you to move the process along.

On days of significance, such as the birth or death of your loved one, you may find yourself experiencing "anniversary grief." It also might be triggered unexpectedly by sights or sounds, for instance, the playing on the radio of a mutual favorite song. It's okay to remember, to recall especially the good times, to smile and cry simultaneously. Prepare for these special days by arranging to be busy, especially with friends and family. The day will move on. There will be a tomorrow.

I knew an upbeat widow who planned two birthday parties for herself in a weekend, one for friends and one for family, because one party couldn't accommodate everybody. With the help of her daughters, she held them outdoors because her apartment wasn't large enough. She enjoyed herself thoroughly. Yet in quieter moments, when the subject of her husband came up, she grew still, tremulous even, as though on the verge of tears. Deep inside she was still grieving.

A friend Connie wrote:

. My husband passed away on my birthday, March 13. After his accident on March 11 as he lay in a hospital bed unresponsive and hooked up to life support, from the moment I first saw him, I knew he wasn't going to make it even though family members told me otherwise, i.e, miracles do happen, he is going to get better, I have to think positive, etc. I also had a strong feeling that he was going to pass away on my birthday which was only two days away, and he did. Alan always bought me something early for my birthday and would put it away until that day came. He had asked me prior to his death what I wanted for my birthday. I told him just give me money. You can do that after being married for so many years, and there were a couple of things I wanted & thought it would be easier for me to go shopping and buy them with the money. After Alan's accident & death, my birthday was the farthest thing from my mind and no way was I in the mood to celebrate it. About one month after he passed, I was looking for something in his closet. I came across a Walgreen's plastic bag. In it was my birthday card with (3) $50 bills inside. The receipt from when he purchased the card was dated one month before he passed away. He wanted to make sure I had something for my birthday. I decided to buy something with the money that would last forever and something to always remember him by. I bought a necklace and ring. Anytime I wear them,

I remember these were the last gifts he bought for my birthday.

Many widows and widowers manage to look good on the outside, but scratch the surface and they still hurt inside. They require ongoing support from family and friends.

Challenge for Change. How lonely are you? On the internet you can find a quiz which you can take to rate your degree of loneliness. If you Google "UCLA Loneliness Scale," you will find half a dozen websites which reprint this quiz.

3. Born Lonely

Language...has created the word loneliness to ex-press the pain of being alone. And it has created the word solitude to express the glory of being alone.
Paul Tillich, Protestant theologian

Definition of lonely. How did you come to this? How did you turn out to be lonely? You can conjecture hypothesis after hypothesis and still not come out with an answer that seems to cover the situation: spouse gone, kids grown, career over, friends moved away or de-ceased. All of these are contributing factors which hap-pen to anyone. Why are some particularly lonely?

You may suffer from loneliness in the same sense as you suffer from physical pain. Using imaging tech-niques to examine how the brain processes pain, research has demonstrated that experiences such as loneliness, os-tracism, and social exclusion have the same effect on the brain.

One way to look at loneliness is to define it as the difference between how much social interaction you ex-perience and how much you feel you need. What is the expectation vs. actuality?

Consider a different example of need. Three popu-lar vehicles have the following gas tank capacities:

Volkswagen Jetta	13.2 gallons
Cadillac Escalade	31 gallons
Ford F-150	23 gallons

If the Jetta had 11 gallons in its tank, it would be nearly full. If the Cadillac had 28 gallons in its tank, it would also be nearly full. But if the F-150 had 11 gallons in its tank, it would be more than half-empty.

In each instance in the diagram below, the left-hand column represents the total capacity of the gas tank while the right represents how much gas is in it at the moment.

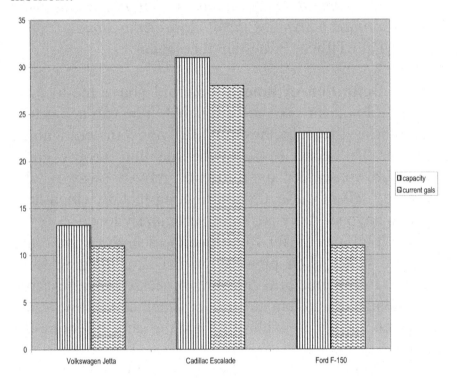

The Ford F-150 is shown to be less full than the other two vehicles, even though it has the same amount of gas as the Volkswagen Jetta.

People capacity. The same principle applies to people and loneliness. It's not just how much companionship you get, but also how much you are expecting. Suppose we can measure the Need For People in NFP units. Consider four people:

	Need For People	People Units Get
Stanley	3 NFP	2.8 PU
Lizzie	11 NFP	10 PU
Myrtle	11 NFP	10 PU
Ted	6 NFP	2.5 PU

Loner: Stanley has a fairly low NFP. He might be considered something of a loner, but he is happy with that. He enjoys woodworking projects and he takes long walks. Sometimes he converses with his neighbors or his kids. He only gets 2.8 People Units, but it is sufficient because it nearly fulfills his Need For People. Stanley rarely feels lonely.

Socialite: Lizzie has a high NFP. She satisfies it by being active in her community. She belongs to three organizations where she meets people. She exchanges phone numbers. She goes to civic activities. Lizzie is usually around people or on the phone with them. She gets 10 People Units to satisfy her high Need For People.

Myrtle also has a high NFP. She lives in a residential care facility and gets around it by propelling her wheelchair with her feet. Anywhere that people gather, like the activity room, you can find Myrtle chatting with people. She stops by the door of residents' rooms to say hello. Myrtle maintains 10 People Units to fit her high Need For People.

Lonely person: Ted has a fairly high NFP, but he doesn't get enough People Units to satisfy it. At those times when he feels his Need For People but has no people around him, he feels lonely. The gap between his NFP and his PU is causing his loneliness. Two possible solutions:

1. Decrease the Need For People. Take the lonely time and turn it into meaningful solitude, a time

when one welcomes being alone. Take up a hobby or activity, or just enjoy the solitude.

2. Increase the People Units. Find ways to include other people. Go where they are. Strike up conversations. Be open to growing a relationship into a friendship.

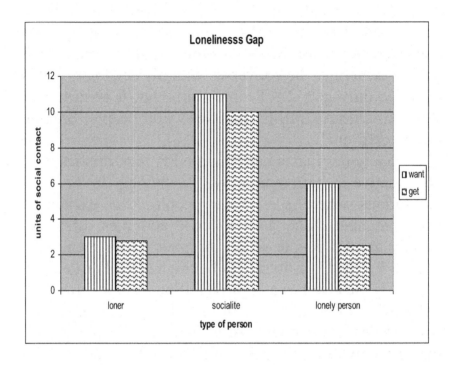

By doing these two things, the left column lowers as the right column rises, and the difference between them (the loneliness gap) decreases. More on how to make these changes as we continue into the book.

Nature or nurture. Scientists often ask the question "is it nature or nurture?" when looking at a human characteristic. Was a person born this way, or was he shaped by his environment? In the case of loneliness, it is both.

Some of us are literally born lonely. Through studies with twins and other research, scientists have

found a particular gene or cluster of genes which deter-
mines predisposition to the characteristic trait of loneliness.

Genetic predisposition. Genes are pieces of the
ribbon of the DNA. There are approximately 30,000 sets
of genes in each segment of DNA in each cell. Each gene
has two parts, one from the father and one from the
mother. Thus a unique person is created carrying some of
the genetic predispositions of each parent.

Genes are instructions for the body. Genes determine whether eyes are brown or blue. They can carry a
predisposition for certain illnesses. That is why a doctor
asks for a family history. Carrying a predisposition does
not necessarily mean that you will get that illness.

Behavioral characteristics have also been shown to
come from genetic make-up. People with a particular
gene or set of genes tend to behave in ways that increase
their chances that they will be lonely.

Nature. Lonely people tend to be introverts if not
downright shy in interacting with other people.

You have the tendency not to go to gatherings of
other people, be it a church potluck or a civic beautifica-
tion committee or a knitting group at the yarn shop. You
know it is important to get out and meet people, but you
tell yourself that this time doesn't feel right. Maybe next
time.

You have a tendency not to initiate conversations
with strangers. As a result, you meet fewer people and
have fewer social contacts to call on when you are lonely.

The other day I was sitting on the bench in front of
the apartment building waiting for the van transport service to pick me up. A woman who lived in the building
sat next to me. Her knees hurt, and she had to rest before
continuing inside. She showed me the scars.

With her leading the conversation, we talked about the heat of course, the neighbors, the building, the corner grocery. It was a lovely conversation that helped pass the time. I wish to imitate her in getting the conversational ball rolling with strangers

Overcoming genetic predispositions. Genetic predispositions can be overcome. There appears to be a genetic tendency toward music. Some people are born musical geniuses. Mozart played keyboard and violin and composed music by the age of five. I started taking music lessons at age seven and learned Every Good Boy Deserves Fun, a mnemonic for EGBDF or the notes on the lines of the treble staff. I plunked along with no particular talent, but I practiced daily. I have not been invited to Carnegie Hall. I can't sit down at a piano in a bar and play melody after melody for the amusement of the patrons. I can get out sheet music and credibly entertain myself. I may not have a gene for music, but by working at it, I have developed sufficient prowess.

Senior center. Deciding that I had to at least try to make some social contacts, I decided to go to lunch at the senior center one day a week. The city van picked up a dozen of us all headed for the center. Others drove, walked, or were brought by family. We arrived at 11. Lunch was at 11:30. We paid $2.50 at the door, our names were checked off, and we were given a lunch ticket.

At first it was all very strange, round tables with six chairs each, total strangers sprinkled among the tables. As the morning progressed the crowd filled in until the room was about two-thirds full.

It only took a few weeks to identify the power table. Open and outgoing, many of them turned in their chairs to greet other diners, but they were that sixth-grade clique all grown up. If there was a vacancy at the table, they were expecting June to come later. Across the room the social table had its regular members, but there were usually a couple of seats left for grabs.

Since it was early, I usually sat at an unoccupied table and hoped that someone would join me. I soon discovered the serving tray of free doughnuts in the back by the coffee, and I took one to nibble while I was sitting alone so it would look like I had something to do. After a couple of months two other women usually came along pretty consistently, and the Avon woman stopped by for a spell. Sometimes others would join us as well.

Food was good, and there was a lot of it: an entrée, veggies, salad, bread and butter. The carb was often barley. I suspect it was government surplus. Fresh fruit or cake for dessert. Milk. Many people brought plastic leftover dishes and took some home for supper.

Then it was time to clear the plate back at the kitchen door and ride the van home. The feeling of strangeness at the center quickly wore off. People began to greet me by name, and I often knew their names as well. It took several months, but the center actually began to feel like a friendly place, one that I looked forward to with warmth. I have not yet made the kind of friendships wherein one makes contact outside the center, but I consider it an important part of my life. I now go twice a week and I have a regular table to sit at.

Nurture. And what impact does our environment have? In your earliest infancy, you were totally dependent on someone to see to your basic needs. Did this person respond to your earliest smiles? If totally unrewarded, your smiles came less often. Even as infants people without proper emotional support start to withdraw.

Infancy. I was born with a small medical condition that needed correcting. Although the condition itself was minor and not life-threatening, I was in discomfort and at times pain for the first year of my life. Did that have an impact on my willingness to trust people in later life?

I only knew about it because it left a physical scar, and at some point I asked. How many are there who have no physical scar and yet, unbeknownst to them, had a rough introduction to life?

Childhood. As you grew, especially in your pre-school years, were you praised for what good you did? Criticized for what you did wrong? For many it was a balance of some of both. A hypercritical parent can be damaging to a child's ego. Some few children suffered the unspeakable trauma of actual abuse. Also rejection and bullying on the playground may have had repercussions.

All of these had an impact on your early development which may have lasted through to your adult years. You may have had early feelings that you were wrong or that you have been abandoned. If unresolved, these carry over to your adult personality.

Adult. Because of your genetic component and your life experiences, you may have developed a more introspective attitude to life. You feel defensive in your responses. When you feel threatened, you experience fear, the body's protective flight-or-fight response. Introversion looks like shyness, but it is different. An introvert may want times of solitude, while a shy person finds socializing difficult even though her inner wish is to connect. An extrovert on the other hand is action-oriented and looks forward to spending time with people.

We all need friends, partners, family, confidants, or other associates, if possible people who love unconditionally. Feelings of loneliness in extreme can lead to poor choices such as drug use, gambling, unwanted sexual risks, eating disorders, or even suicide. Loneliness is known to be as threatening to health as cigarette smoking or obesity.

One option is to get outside help in cognitive retraining to change expectations and to enhance potential for social contact. You test the validity of your first feelings. Above all you can learn to stop blaming yourself for what isn't your fault.

My family didn't hug. My husband's family did, and I soon picked up the habit. One time when my husband and baby Susie and I were visiting from the East Coast, it fell to my husband's mom and dad to drive us from their house in Detroit to my mother's house in Cincinnati. They spent the night. Upon their departure, there were hugs all around. After they left my mother commented, "That's kind of nice, this hugging thing. I don't know why we never did it." From that time on my family hugged on coming and going.

Affectionate behavior is a reciprocal thing. If one person extends some sign of affection such as a hug, the other person is likely to respond in kind. A hug boosts levels of the bonding hormone oxytocin. That may lead to less stress, a stronger immune system, and even lower blood pressure.

Inheriting your person. For the purpose of analogy, consider your person as the house you grew up in. Suppose your parents didn't care for this house properly because they didn't know how, and they had other priorities, maybe civic involvement, maybe alcohol. (This correlates to upbringing.) It was not structurally sound to begin with. (This correlates to genetic predisposition.)

Eventually you have inherited the house. The roof leaks. The sink in one of the bathrooms is backed up. The wallpaper is peeling. Several windows are cracked. It is a mess.

But you have inherited it. You have a choice. You can blame its condition on your parents as you sit and listen to the water dripping from the ceiling into the pots on the floor. Or you can decide that it is your house now, and you have the choice to fix it up. It will require an expenditure of time, energy, and money. You must be committed to the project or it will fail. But you can make it your house, if not a showcase, at least livable. The past is past. It is your house now.

So it is with your being. Whatever interactions you may have had in the past, even though they shaped you at the time, are no longer attributable to others. You must move on. You must assume responsibility for your being and fix it up as best you can.

Challenge for Change. Think of a friendly comment, perhaps for encountering a person in an elevator or in the grocery line. Examples:

It is {hot/cold/windy} today.

I like your {blouse/shoes/tie}.

Did you hear how the {Reds/Patriots/Lakers} did last night?

You can use these or come up with something better. Have your comment ready, and try it sometime.

4. Self-Esteem

If your compassion does not include yourself, it is incomplete.
Buddha

Self-esteem, an inner light that shines through, tells people that you value yourself and that you are a person to be valued. It illuminates your person. Without that inner light, you recede into the background.

You can develop positive self-esteem by listening to your inner messages. Your thoughts control your self-esteem

A love affair. When you are alone with yourself, do you spend your time with someone you like? Do you feel comfortable with yourself as with a friend? Do you accept yourself as a person?

If you answer in the negative, as many do, then your alone-time will suffer. When alone with yourself, it should at least be someone for whom you have a high regard. You are worthwhile.

Dissing yourself. When you make a mistake, do you call yourself stupid? You meant to pay with a debit card but handed over your credit card. Now a household expense will be logged into the wrong place unless you make a notation on the credit card statement. What a bother. How stupid. You say to yourself, "I make me so angry."

You have catastrophized from the idea of doing something stupid to finding that you are stupid in general. Maybe "stupid" represents a trigger word that brings up feelings of shame. The word "careless" fits better. "I did a careless thing. Next time I will be more careful." It is not a big deal.

Maybe when you grew up you were yelled at for spilling milk. (Most of us were.) Now that nobody yells at you, then you do it to yourself.

When I was four, my mother left me alone with a package of Oreos. I was allowed to have two for a snack. Instead I twisted apart the cookies and scraped off the filling with my teeth. I put the cookie pieces on the table and twisted apart another cookie. By the time my mother came back, I had a row of a dozen outsides neatly lined up on the table. Yes, I got yelled at. "How could you?" she shouted. I didn't know. I just started and didn't stop. Since she was yelling at me, I felt ashamed, assumed I was bad.

To be fair, my mother did not ordinarily yell at me. Sometimes I inadvertently pushed her buttons, as I did with teachers and other authority figures. My Sunday School teacher called me "ornery." In growing up, I probably experienced a fair number of adults who wanted to put me in my place.

That is how the adult person learns to supply the internal criticism which is no longer present externally. You beat up on yourself because you feel that is what the situation calls for. Worse yet, you have become a perfectionist. You have the feeling that without that negative voice keeping after you, then you would become worthless and dissolute. You feel it prompts you to succeed.

What it does is to cause you a lot of anxiety. It causes you to get flustered, so that when it comes time to pull out the debit or the credit card, you get confused.

Image. Self-esteem involves images of how you see yourself as a person: your beliefs and thought processes your emotions, your interactions, your appearance, and your behaviors. You have a sense of your self-worth, whether high or low.

Low self-esteem can be debilitating. Risks for low self-esteem can be influenced by financial status, position in community, marginalized people, and age. Self-esteem drops rapidly after 60 years of age. Women tend toward lower self-esteem.

Process. A simple three-step process will go a long way in helping you to improve your self-esteem.

Step 1. Recognize the toxic thought. During a late-night rumination, pondering the meaning of life and the happenstance of circumstance, I was overwhelmed by the thought, "I love the world." I didn't know what I meant—the geographic structure with all its natural beauty or the civilization in all its complexity or the people so alike and so different.

Immediately I recognized the negative voice that comes in such situations. "You love the world? Are you kidding me? You're a curmudgeon. You're not the type to love the world." That negative voice threatened to take over my feelings.

Step 2. Dispute the thought. What type does it take? So often I have heard such critical feelings, those put-downs, and listened to them. I don't know where they come from, but this time I wasn't buying into them.

Step 3. Affirm the positive. "I do too. I can love the world." I still don't know what that means, but I an encouraged to think that I am a person who loves the world.

Another voice. My friend Libby writes:

Learning to Love Ourselves
That can be journey fraught with
Hills and Mountains to climb

But at the summit
Peace and Calm, a Contentment
Many of us have but only dreamed to feel

If we had it we have now lost it
Perhaps some of us have never felt it
But.... all of us can achieve it

Will it be easy--I doubt it
Will we need to drown out that which plays in our
heads
Of course
Will we need to walk away from toxic people and
places
We will

Drowning out...
If only it was as easy as just dunking our head
But alas....it is not
It is a constant state of work

Can we handle it
Yes we can
Just knowing you have taken the time
To read this
Think about this
Taken it to heart
Proves you are courageous enough
To put all you have learned
Into play

Another example. This three-step process can work for any negative thoughts. Believe in your self-worth. For example, suppose my negative inner thought is that I am fat. (I have been.) Note I do not use pretty words like overweight or heavy. When we are talking about critical thoughts, the word that comes to mind is fat.

Step 1. Recognize the toxic thought. I couldn't dispute that my body mass index was higher than it should be. As I stepped into my size 22 jeans, I was concerned that people saw me as fat.

Step 2. Dispute the thought. When I walk into a roomful of people, they don't turn away in disgust. What they are not seeing or judging is whether I am fat. By my physical appearance, they recognize and greet my inner person.

Step 3. Affirm the positive. My inner person is a person of worth. All humans have worth. I have something to offer the people in the room, if only by my presence.

It will take time, but work on your negative thoughts as they arise. I displayed all the signs of low self-esteem, of being afraid to put myself forth. My handwriting is small. My voice is soft. I dress down. I still do, but now I can say I am more at peace with myself, that I have reconciled many of the negative self-images.

Thoughts. Self-esteem is based on your thoughts, your inner voices that judge or affirm you. In low self-esteem, your inner voice becomes the toxic critic that won't allow you to feel good about yourself.

Even if you do the same thing in the same way the next time, don't beat up on yourself. Take a positive attitude by saying: (1) next time I really will do it differently, or (2) it isn't that important.

It's your mind. You tell it what to do. Be assertive.

Help. If you still have low self-esteem, then the time has come for outside help to break the patterns. Through the practice of cognitive behavioral therapy, many therapists turn the process of raising self-esteem around in weeks or at most a few months, not the protracted process of years of intensive psychotherapy. Seek out a counselor, tell him your goals, and ask about his course of therapy. When you have found a fit, make an appointment. In spite of your anxiety and misgivings, keep that appointment. You are on the way to a new, more productive, and more valid appraisal of self.

Rejection. Social or professional rejection can cause negative feelings of "not good enough." Possibly you didn't meet someone else's standards, whether realistic or not. Perhaps the perception of you was not accurate. Perhaps in spite of reasonable standards and accurate perceptions, you simply did not fit the criteria for the relationship or the job. This does not make you less of a person.

Ease up. Your feelings got hurt. That happens. Take time to "pick yourself up and dust yourself off." Take note of the negative thoughts, the internal name-calling, the blame of self or others. Do not see in yourself a bad person or think of them as bad persons. For whatever reason, an opportunity didn't happen. Though disappointed now, you will find other opportunities. Smile.

Humility. In affirming the positive, you are acknowledging to yourself your gifts. Be grateful for them. Honestly recognize your strengths in yourself without flaunting them in front of others.

To deny your talents in your thought processes because it feels vain to admit them is false modesty. The word "vanity" means emptiness. It occurs when you puff yourself up before others to try to gain approval or praise. Humility is internally owning your gifts and using them as appropriate. You don't need others' affirmation because you feel good about yourself.

Being human. The criterion for a person to be lovable is that they are part of the human race. That's all it takes. Ideally you try to love everyone. Some you may not like. Some may have even committed atrocities; in no way are you required to condone or excuse these. Some you may not even feel comfortable with, and you avoid being in their presence. But the general rule is to love everyone in the abstract, to wish them good and positive things in their lives.

That brings us to the central question of loving yourself. You are after all a part of the human race and worthy to be loved. If you reject yourself, how can you hope that others accept you? If you want to be less lonely in your life, you have to give others a chance to embrace you spiritually. They need to see that you value yourself and them also.

Significance. To be less lonely, you must love the world. Aware of all the foibles and injustices and ugliness, you embrace it as the work in progress that it is. You live here. If you disenfranchise yourself from the world, you cut yourself off from its people. You will be lonely.

To love the world, you have to love yourself so that you have the love to give to other people. You can't be open to other people when you are shut down to yourself. In modern psychobabble we call it self-esteem, but that means affirming to the positive in yourself and disallowing the negative. You have to struggle with it continually, but in overcoming the negative in yourself, you learn to discredit negative vibes in others. You can love the world, and the world loves you back.

Challenge for Change. Capture a negative thought, a self put-down. You are never entirely free of them. Challenge it using the three steps outlined above. Lay the thought to rest.

(If you are thinking, "I can't do this," then challenge that thought. Where does it come from? Who says you can't? Now do it.)

5. Solitude

Being solitary is being alone well: being alone luxuriously immersed in doings of your own choice, aware of the fullness of your own presence rather than of the absence of others. Because solitude is an achievement.

Alice Koller in Maitland, Sara, *How To Be Alone,* p. 187.

Solitude. Solitude is time spent alone without feeling lonely. Now that you have a more positive image of yourself, the possibility opens up for you to like being with yourself. You learn to fill the time with internal or external activities of your choice.

We defined loneliness as the gap between the amount of time you spend with social contact and the amount of time you feel you need social contact. "Social scientist researchers define loneliness as the emotional state created when people have fewer social contacts and *meaningful* relationships than they would like."[3] Learning to be comfortable with solitude lessens the time experienced as lonely and shrinks that gap.

You might fear the thought of solitude. It stems from an apprehension of being alone. You question whether being alone can ever feel good. You may be suspicious of others who spend time alone, that they are not quite with the program. When you are lonely, you feel desperate and anxious to overcome your loneliness. You either accept your loneliness or blame yourself. You feel like a banana without a peel.

Planning. Analyze your day. Find the strong times, the active times, the natural breaks. Coincide your

---

[3] *The Week*, Jan. 11, 2019, p. 11,

solitude with your natural body rhythms. Look forward to taking up activities, and look forward to letting go of them.

Take time to reflect. Forgive yourself and others. Express gratitude.

Reverie. You can get lost in lonely, or you can learn to live with lonely and even survive lonely. Fill the time any way you find comfortable. As simplest of all activities, undertake to spend the time in positive thought or reverie. Think of pleasant memories or hopes for the future.

I knew an eighty-year-old woman in assisted living who complained that she found herself spending time each day on the bed staring up at the ceiling. She felt it restful and even pleasant but at the same time she felt it was "wrong" to waste time like that. Once she accepted it as part of her routine, she experienced the time as meaningful. The things we didn't do in our more active years have now become appropriate.

Worry time. Do not allow your quiet time to be taken over by worries and anxieties. Set aside a separate time for problem-solving, to look at what needs to be done or needs to happen and how to get there. Use this time also to consult with others if you cannot find the solutions.

Money and health are the two most common concerns experienced by the elderly. You cam often find resources from your Area Agency on Aging. Call the national network at 202-872-0888 or visit www.n4a.org to get the number for your local Area Agency.

The Area Agency can often identify subsidies such as for utilities for seniors on fixed incomes. They may know of low income housing options. Other programs provide low-cost or free food.

If you have nagging health concerns, call your doctor's office for a phone evaluation. She may want you to come in to rule out something more serious. If your health concerns prevent you from taking care of yourself adequately, ask your Area Agency about a caregiver.

Times of worry are appropriate to try to problem-solve. Turning these worries over to another may be the solution. Also consider involving your family members. Going around and around on the same issues does not help. Address your problems during your worry time, but only then. During your times of solitude, put aside these stressors and concentrate on the positive aspects of your life.

Mind-wandering. I might think about what to get my son for his birthday. His wife buys his socks. He doesn't wear ties. I don't know his taste in music. He reads sci fi, but I know nothing about the genre. So I think of times I have been with him, things I have observed. Perhaps I will ask for hints. The time spent thinking about him has been good.

Ponder the differences between the oceans. The prevailing winds of the North Atlantic push out from the land, and indigo ripples lap the shore. Gulls guard empty strips of sand. Tourists in jackets and mittens drive past on their way to the Old North Church and Faneuil Hall. The horizon offers tangerine sunrises and passing cargo ships.

In So Cal the prevailing winds of the Pacific push the water in to shore, and gray-green rollers crash onto the sand dotted with blankets. Mounds of flesh, held in by scraps of cloth of lime green and hot coral, populate the beach. Gulls guard Igloo coolers. The horizon offers sunsets of magenta swirled with fuchsia and sails of passing catamarans.

That was fun. Or reflect on a wedding that you have attended, what the bride and bridesmaids wore, what you wore, where the reception was, and what food was served. Think about all the details of the day and recall your feelings. Enjoy your reverie.

Movement. Whatever your activity, take breaks for minimal physical activity. When the chair has grown up around you, when the blood has settled to your buttocks, move a bit. Stand in the middle of the room and swing your arms, or do armchair exercises. Go to the window and look out while marching in place. Fuss with a cup of tea, with heating the water and dunking the teabag and adding sugar to taste. Take a break and return to your activity refreshed, or start something new. Appreciate the day as it flows by.

Television. When you plan your day, choose what television programs you will watch. Find programs that absorb your interest, whether they are enlightening or funny or gripping or athletic. Then for the rest of the day, remove yourself from in front of the set unless you are doing something in addition to watching. When it becomes the only input, it loses its entertainment value and may even make you feel more bored, more lonely, similar to nibbling at snacks all day long but never feeling hungry. Some people like it as background for their day, while others turn it off.

Exercise daily. Studies show exercise increases longevity. If you have had physical therapy, dig out the exercise diagrams your therapist gave you and develop a routine. Ask your doctor about exercise. Go online to find exercises that strengthen particular parts of your body. Buy a stationary bike or other exercise equipment and use it. Above all, find the time of your day that works best for you and implement it in your schedule.

My back is in shambles, and I use a walker, but I exercise when I take my morning and evening meds. To put in my eye drops, I lie flat on my back, so I might as well do a routine including leg lifts, lumbar rotations, and other exercises. I also ride an exercise bike while watching DVDs almost daily. These practices are so ingrained in my schedule that I don't notice them.

Walk. If you are able, get out to walk a few times a week. It is the best exercise, whether around the block or to a certain store and back. Notice the landscaping and the storefronts. Look directly at people you pass and say hello to those who meet your gaze. Walk up and down the corridors of your building.

Pets. Most responsive to human attention and most popular are dogs and cats. You can find comfort in stroking an animal on your lap or pleasure in tossing a ball for fetch. All animals eat and poop, and you have to be willing to be responsible for that. A dog is a good excuse for a walk.

My friend Libby writes of solitude:

I find it in the garden
Connecting with the Earth
And Mother Nature

Always with my boys (my cats), My dear Peeka and Boo
The unconditional love of animals is a peace that is unexplainable in words.
It's a feeling, an emotional state, a place of being and connectedness

Often this feeling of Peace and Solitude
Is found in my imagination

I forgo the sounds of Cars passing by
To just focus on Mother Nature
Blowing Gently and Rustling the tree across the way

Watching the hanging plant
Moving so slightly from the corner of my balcony
The wind chime above swaying back and forth

I question is this Serenity
Or Nature hypnotizing
My eyes to close, my soul to sleep

This aloneness, this quiet space
Alone with my thoughts
Shattered like cheap glass
When life's reality knocks at my mind's door
Reminding me I must dress
And Leave all this behind

One must make Their Alone Time A
Blessed and Beautiful Time
Before it transposes into a time Of Loneliness

Feel your breath
Listen to your heart
Be at ease

Rejuvenate with a walk
Energize by playing In the garden
Fill empty space with moments of joy

Stay above ground
Don't allow yourself

To sink too far down

Just float
Find peace

Other activities. So many possibilities abound that I am devoting Chapters 7-9 to them. If you can go out, then get out a few times a week. If you cannot go out, then choose from activities that can be done from home. Either way, involve yourself so that you have less time to feel lonely.

Self-knowledge. "To move from loneliness to solitude is to recover the world we have lost."[4] You make conscious choices following your own sense of appropriateness about how you are to proceed through each day. You discover yourself. You learn what is in your inner being. Most great art—visual, literary, musical—involved some period of solitude. Finding what is within you enables you to bring it to others.

Challenge for Change. Make a loose schedule for today or tomorrow. Set mealtimes, bedtimes, and exercise times. If you have opportunities for social contact, in person or by phone, pencil them in. Arrange your solitary activities around these anchors.

---

[4] Dumm, Thomas, *Loneliness as a Way of Life*, p. 40.

6. Meditation and Mindfulness

Drop by drop is the water pot filled. Likewise, the wise man, gathering it little by little, fills himself with good.
Buddha, *Dhammapada*

Loneliness can cause anxiety, and the practice of meditation can bring calm. Therefore the subject of meditation is appropriate for a book on loneliness. It gives you one more option for dealing with the pain.

Disclaimer. One can learn to read music. Middle C is a symbol below the lines and corresponds to a certain key on the piano. Yet one may practice and practice and practice some more, becoming quite adept at selected concertos, but still not have learned everything about making music from this cabinet of keys.

So too I have read about and dabbled in the practice of meditation but do not have the lifetime of discoveries and experiences to draw on to be able to tell you about it. The best I can do is to describe my research. I want to give you enough of an overview of what meditation is so that you can decide if you want to pursue it further.

Whole books take up the subject, and you are encouraged to explore these if at all interested. Some people join a meditation group or have a meditation coach, not only at the beginning but as a lifelong experience if they desire.

Background. Meditation is cross-cultural and comes to us in many forms; indeed the major religions of the world all have one or more traditions of meditation, some of them hundreds of years old.

Along with the various practices of meditation are the bodies of teaching associated with the individual cultures: for example, the sayings of Buddha, the Bhagavad Gita in India. You can successfully practice meditation with or without looking into these teachings.

Benefits. Adherents claim such benefits as sharpening the mind, increasing emotional well-being, promoting calmness, and developing spiritual insights. American Tibetan Buddhist Pema Chödrön wrote, "I personally feel that the ultimate reason why we practice, why we listen to these teachings, why we try to bring this into every moment of our life, is so that we can become completely loving people."[5]

Time. Although you may want to purchase a yoga cushion, no special equipment is needed. A comfy chair and a quiet space will do. The essential component lies in the commitment of time, preferably the same time every day. Once you have started, there should be no "zero" days. You can move around the schedule—early morning or midafternoon or whatever—until you find the best fit, but you shouldn't go to bed without having meditated for the day.

How long depends on the individual. Some start with eight minutes and work up to what feels right, maybe twenty minutes or an hour. Even a smaller investment of time will bring some benefit. I set the timer on the microwave for ten minutes. As I practice, it seems to go more quickly.

Posture. Your posture should be relaxed, seated on a chair or on the floor or lying down. Your back

---

[5] Pema Chödrön, *How To Meditate*, p. 172.

should be straight. I use an unconstrained posture that is as straight as my back goes naturally. If on a chair you can be cross-legged or have your feet on the floor. You should not experience unnecessary strain in any part of your body. Your hands are quiet, resting on your legs palms up or in a prayer position.

Breathing. Essential to meditation, one inhales and exhales evenly. Focus your attention on your breathing. Usually you take a deep breath in through your nostrils, and exhale slowly either through mouth or nostrils. (I've read of either.) Concentrate on your breathing.

Count out rhythms of inhaling and exhaling; for example, inhale to the count of four and exhale to the count of five. Do what is comfortable. Typically the exhale is longer than the inhale, which means the inhale is sharper than the exhale.

Thoughts. If a thought pops up to distract you (and many will), quietly address it and dismiss it, perhaps to dissimilate it in a great blue sky that you imagine above your head. The function of the meditating is not to be completely without thoughts, but to recognize that they have appeared, become aware of them, and then put them aside, bringing the focus back to the breathing.

Some people focus on a mantra, a single syllable or word heard in the back of the head in unison with the breathing. Some common mantras: om, Abba, any color, Jesus. One can merely label thoughts that occur as "thinking" and return to the breathing.

Thoughts are not judged as good or bad, nor are you to become discouraged that a thought has arisen. Meditation accepts us just as we are. With practice the mind will become better trained. Meditation lies not in being completely without thoughts, but in recognizing them nonjudgmentally and returning to the breath.

The Catholic mystic St. Teresa of Avila compares progress in the Prayer of Quiet with watering a garden. At first it is watered by fetching buckets of water from the well, laborious but effective. As time goes on one is able to draw the water using a windlass (an apparatus used for moving heavy weights). In the next stage, a brook runs through the garden.

In the last and final stage rain soaks the ground involving no effort from you. Meditation becomes that easy, that natural. You are not to be discouraged if the phase of drawing water from the well seems to take a long time, or even if the well is sometimes dry, but are to visit it repeatedly until more water flows.[6]

Other options. In some meditations I can choose to do a body scan. Starting with my toes and working up to feet, legs, torso, head, I become aware of each body part in succession, flexing and releasing, holding that awareness for a few seconds and moving on. It leaves me with a relaxed feeling.

Some schools of meditation offer thoughts on which to reflect during the meditation. For example in the metta, you begin by befriending yourself. Classically four phases are repeated:

o May I be free from danger.
o May I have mental happiness.
o May I have physical happiness.
o May I have ease of well-being.[7]

In guided meditation, either from a teacher or some form of media, a calm voice walks you through a meditative process. To find recordings of guided meditations, google "guided meditation" or enter it on the search engine on YouTube.com. Some meditations can

---

[6] St. Teresa of Avila, *The Life of Teresa of Jesus*, p. 128.
[7] Sharon Salzberg, *Lovingkindness*, pp. 29-30.

be purchased while others are free. You can experiment with what is available until you find one or more that suit you in content and length.

If you continue to practice meditation, you may want to go more deeply into the teachings. In the many traditions, you will become acquainted with a new philosophy of life. Research to find that tradition which brings you a sense of well-being. You can explore it for a lifetime and never finish.

My friend Halbert, who is an experienced practitioner of meditation, writes:

> In his 2005 commencement address at Kenyon College, David Foster Wallace told this story: "There are these two young fish swimming along, and they happen to meet an older fish swimming the other way, who nods at them and says, "Morning, boys, how's the water?" And the two young fish swim on for a bit, and then eventually one of them looks over at the other and goes, 'What the hell is water?' "

> Wallace went on to say, "It is about simple awareness--awareness of what is so real and essential, so hidden in plain sight all around us, that we have to keep reminding ourselves, over and over: 'This is water, this is water.'"

> We swim in the ocean of our minds continuously and meditation is a tool for reminding ourselves "this is how it is" and learning about its currents and tidal movements; its warm parts and its cool parts. "This is my mind. This.is how it works. This is how I can lead it more workably."

Meditation is an ancient practice and many people have talked about their experience of meditation and its benefits. In the last fifty years, scientists have conducted research on it and among many others, meditation has been shown to produce :

- integration of the seemingly different parts of us
- a sense of calmness that becomes available even when not meditating
- increased self-awareness
- reduced stress
- a less frantically busy mind
- an increased capacity for concentration
- reduced sense of loneliness.

Loneliness has been shown to be reduced through the very practice of meditation. In addition, there are many urban areas where meditation groups are available.

Mindfulness. The practice of concentrating on the breathing during your meditation is in itself mindfulness, but the term can also mean simply being present to the here and now—the sights, sounds, smells, tastes of the present moment. Put aside all worries about the future, all regrets about the past, indeed all thoughts. They are neither good nor bad. Focus on the present. "Mindfulness is the basic human ability to be fully present, aware of where we are and what we're doing, and not overly reactive or overwhelmed by what's going on around us." [www.mindul.org/.../ mindfulness-getting-started]

Mindfulness is "a simple way to become more grounded in the present moment and develop a nonjudgmental awareness about how your body and mind work."[8]

For example, I focus on the person about to approach me on the sidewalk. Will we meet eyes and exchange a greeting, or will he refuse to acknowledge me? Place no judgment on it. It just is. I let my thoughts move to the next experience.

I listen to the motorcycle as it passes by on the street: a roar increasing to a crescendo, a pause while the motorcyclist switches gears, another roar and even higher crescendo. I listen to the silence when it is gone, the chirping of the birds, a distant car horn.

I feel the breeze on my face, a bit too chilly for this time of year but bracing. I feel the warmth of my jacket, the pounding sensation of my feet on the pavement. I smell the cinnamon rolls from a bakery I am passing, the diesel of the bus picking up passengers. Stopping at Starbucks, I order a latte. The world can become a place of wonder when I embrace it sense by sense.

Jon Kabat-Zinn, founding Executive Director of the Center for Mindfulness, has developed an eight-week evidence-based program Mindfulness-Based Stress Reduction (MBSR). It has been used effectively in hospitals, schools, corporations, prisons, and professional sports. [www.mindfulnesscds.com.] If you hear of it being offered, you might look into it.

Alternatives. Adherents of meditation claim it brings calm and even happiness. I have read and reflected on scripture twice a day for many years and feel that brings some of the same benefits. Others pray the rosary daily. Still others reflect on the Twelve Steps, an infinite-

[8] Giovanni Dienstmann, *Practical Meditation*, p. 82.

ly rich set of principles. Cultures like the Native Americans have their own practices. The point is that the mind can be trained to work to better advantage. Meditation provides one step-by-step process for doing that.

Challenge for Change. Set the timer on the microwave and try it.

7. Activities at Home

When I knit, everything else vanishes. Sadness, anxiety, anger, confusion. It is just me and the yarn and the lovely sound of my needles clicking together.
"10 things i learned from knitting," Ann Hood, knitting *yarns*, Ann Hood, ed.

Overview. This chapter aims to find ways to make lonely time fulfilling. To that end various possibilities are listed, more than any one person needs. Some of these suggestions will be relevant to you now. Read the major subheadings to decide which intrigue you. Add your own ideas in the margin.

Make that first move to transform your time. Get started on something. Later when you have tried some things on your first list, dig the book out again and take another look. You may find something new that appeals to you at this time.

Whatever it is, put yourself into it. If you are rearranging the photo album, look at each photo with interest. Plan on showing the completed album to a sibling. If you are baking, criss-cross the peanut butter cookies with a fork. If you are knitting, count your stitches.

Your life consists in these activities, so enjoy. Lists upon lists. Ideas upon ideas. How to occupy the inner part of yourself? How to spend your time alone so that it doesn't feel lonely? In this chapter I describe activities that you can try when you are at home. Most of these should work even if you are shut-in, although you may have to ask someone to pick up items for you.

Computer. If you have access to a computer, you will be able to research any and all ideas. Investigate the advantages of desktop, laptop, notebook for your personal use. I have seen advertisements for simpler-to-use computers designed especially for seniors, but I don't know what the trade-offs are. If at all possible, find a family member or friend who can advise and instruct you.

Many libraries have free computers. Sometimes the staff is willing to help you get started. Your residence may have public computers. Be careful what you save (never financial information or account numbers); people can find a way to hack into it.

Search engines. You can spend a lot of time entering things into search engines like Google and following the suggestions. Broccoli. Antarctica. Dolly Madison. Lyme tic disease.

One day I decided to put it to the test and entered 1949 Rose Bowl. The entire game (Northwestern vs. California) was available filmed by one camera with one lens up on the sidelines. Unlike modern broadcasts with multiple camera angles and replays, the single camera followed the quarterback as he dropped back to pass, made a high arc of the ball's progress, and focused on the nest of possible receivers. NU won 20-14. Try googling something unusual.

Reading. The most fundamental of activities, reading involves going places while sitting in an armchair. Fiction or nonfiction or both? Mystery or romance or history? You can select your genre, or you can read whatever comes your way

Start with your own bookshelves. Find books that you haven't yet read, and set them on a table to look over. Some you are not interested in ever reading. Those can go out. Someone will like them. Pick one book that looks good, set it aside, and reshelve the rest in a separate section to make it easier to grab the next.

Now sort the other books. Determine which you may want to reread someday, especially classics. Sometimes after I've reread a book, I give it away, knowing I won't read it a third time. I want to keep them all, but I have too many others and need the space.

Some books didn't entertain the first time. No point in keeping them. Reference books may or may not have relevance for your current situation.

Already you have spent an afternoon or more in sorting through your books. You have earned the right to knock off and read the one you picked out.

If you live in an institutional setting, your residence may have space in the activity room or a library for discarded books. Not only is it a place to take yours, but it is an endless source of reading materials.

Expand beyond your own books. Your library may have an online catalog. Use it to find books that interest you. If you can't go out, see if you can find someone to get you your own library card and then pick up and return books for you. Some libraries operate a bookmobile.

Look into electronic books (e-books) like Kindle. You don't need a computer to use this. New books and releases are offered for sale, but there are also bargain and even free books to download.

Subscribe to a newspaper or magazine, new fodder for your mind on a daily, weekly, or monthly basis. Pick up a copy of the free town news tabloid that is left in the lobby of your building. Read classic religious works. If you have a computer, take an on-line learning course or listen to TED talks. Look things up on Wikipedia, and follow the hyperlinks to new topics.

What to watch. Choose your screen time to fit your schedule and tastes. You can watch something currently airing on cable or on a network.

Binge-watch an entire television series or old Cary Grant movies. Professional and college sports are available any season of the year. Play with your remote and find out what all the buttons do and undo.

Browse YouTube.com. When you open, it will show currently trending views in a screen. If you scroll over the screen, it will often play a few seconds of the clip. The amount of time the clip takes is shown in the bottom right corner. You can enter any item you want in the search engine at the top. View clips of specific sporting events, Saturday Night Live, episodes from the Mickey Mouse clubhouse, a Mozart symphony, or recent discussions of the Chinese economy. Search also for how-tos, cartoons, documentaries, items that people have uploaded (pets, bloopers, travel) and favorite musical artists.

Or turn the electronics off for an evening or longer.

Watch the clouds, seeing how white cumulus dotting the sky make shapes. They draw toward each other and pull back again, creating a drama of whether they will touch. Eventually they kiss, and two small clouds become one larger cloud. As you watch, the sky becomes covered in pearly gray, rumply like God's blanket.

Watch the sidewalk and the street. See who comes into and goes out of the building across the street.

Watch the stars rise and set. Get a star map and learn to identify constellations.

Listening. Music soothes the soul. Play your own music on CDs or LPs, or listen on the radio. Play an instrument if you have one tucked in the closet. Mine is an accordion. Find new music on Pandora or Spotify. Sing to yourself.

Listen to talk radio or pod casts. I have three radio stations on preset, general talk, sports talk, and religious.

Writing. If you prefer to write to yourself, keep a journal of any style, any content. Write about what you did today or more importantly about what you thought about today. Experiment with stream-of-consciousness in which you keep your pen moving as fast as you can with whatever comes to mind. Do not censor yourself.

If you like, add items to your journal such as a picture your grandkid drew, a photo, a note. Let it be your space to create, remember, contemplate, or reflect. I know a person who calls her journal her "calm space." Mine is more my struggle space where I work things out.

Keep a commonplace book, a cross between a journal and a scrapbook. Record in it your memories and reflections, and tape or paste to it anything flat that will enhance these entries—a ticket stub, a special birthday card or note, a photograph, a newspaper article, a leaf pressed between two pieces of waxed paper, a scrap of ribbon or material, a recipe or menu. Use different colored pens and vary the pages, creating a work of art of each.

At the top of each page of your commonplace book, put a title and the date the entry was written. Leave a few pages blank at the front to list the titles, thus creating a table of contents. Many people find an 8 ½ x 11 spiral notebook or a three-ring binder to work best. Over the years you will accumulate a whole shelf of commonplace books. Thomas Jefferson did.

Write a letter to the editor of your local newspaper or a magazine. Include a phone number so that it can be verified. Write to your Congressional Representative and

Senator. They do keep track of how their mail is running on issues. Write your state assembly person or the city council. Write the President. If you want your voice to be heard, then speak out.

Have a separate steno pad just for lists. Every day or so stretch your brain by listing as much of something as you can—types of mammals or birds or flowers, states and capitals, Broadway plays, types of canned soup, whatever comes to mind. Even make a list of things you can make lists of. Country singers. Mystery authors. Shirts in your closet (without looking). States or countries you have been to. Things in your purse or pockets. Students in your classes at school (any level).Things you have lost. Things you do when bored. Goals for the year.

Make a list for each letter of the alphabet. For example, a list of colors might start with **A**zure, **B**lue, **C**anary. List fruits: **A**pricot, **B**anana, **C**antaloupe.

Make an observation notebook. Note everything you see, hear, touch, taste, and smell. Observe as if for the first time the wooden end table, the gray coffee mug on the wooden end table, the chip on the gray coffee mug on the wooden end table. Smell the lingering aroma of the coffee. Feel the smoothness of the wood. Listen to the garbage truck picking up dumpsters on the road outside. Be present to the moment, not the past, not the future, but what is in your experience right now. Jot it down. If you can, go to different places, a park or a mall and write down what is present.

Perhaps you will use your observations in a screenplay you are writing. These days some people are turning to screenplays as a vehicle for their expressions because they are more familiar with that mode of communicating. Learn the rules for formatting your endeavor, and consider specialized software to assist you.

Make a gratitude list of things in the day for which you give thanks: a fresh banana, a nod from someone you passed, a dear memory. The list differs each day. You can keep it in a notebook or give thanks for the items on the list and discard it. Be confident you will have new items for your gratitude list tomorrow.

Write out your bucket list of things you want to do before you kick the bucket. Be sure to see the movie of the same name. Your list doesn't have to be as far-reaching.

Dream of things and write them down. Plan a dream vacation. Fantasize about opening a business. Design your dream home: how many rooms, what amenities in the bath, what family and friends you will invite.

Keep paper and pen handy; learn to use your computer if you have one. Consider inexpensive voice recognition software that allows you to speak your words directly into text up on the computer. Look in your app store.

The major forms of creative writing include fiction, nonfiction, and poetry, although these broad categories overlap sometimes. Like Emily Dickinson, you may write on scraps of brown wrapping paper and old envelopes. If you want to save it, you may store it in a binder or a computer file. How much time you want to spend polishing it is up to you.

You may want to share it in its final form with family or friends. Let them in on your creative side.

If you decide to publish, check magazines you read for submission information. The library has resource books on where and how to submit manuscript. While at the library, ask if they know of a local writing group.

With your cell phone make a video of your grand-kids, or flower-arranging, or the county fair. Save it and show it to others. Post it on YouTube.

Networking. Communicate with family and friends through phone, e-mail, personal letters and cards. If in a residence, visit the activity room. Keep notes so that the next time you are in touch, you can ask how that cataract surgery went.

Meditation. Tips on meditation and mindfulness are in chapter 6. Some people make it part of their daily routine. Also consider yoga.

Computer games. These can be fun, but these can be addictive as well, especially the search-and-destroy games that teens play. Devotees pay money to sit in an audience watching gamers' actions on a big screen.

Older games like PacMan are making a comeback. Tetris never died.

My favorite is Mahjongg, a tile-matching game. I play that every evening while my dinner is in the micro-wave. Possibly it helps maintain cognitive skills.

Board games and card games such as Monopoly, Risk, bridge, and checkers can be played online against the computer using Artificial Intelligence. If you have the physical board game, you can set up two tokens and play against yourself. Many forms of solitaire can be played on the computer or with a real deck of cards. The physi-cal feel of shuffling is nice in this modernized world. Jig-saw puzzles and crossword puzzles can be done either on the computer or by hand.

Family history. You hold the old stories, the leg-ends, and the family background. Document that in a manner you can share with the next generations. Start a journal of memories, either in a notebook or on the com-puter. Tales on the computer are easier to arrange chronologically, but random works also. Include an approximate date (the year) or time references (when Joey was two).

Record your memories, especially of their growing-up years. Your personal style from within the pages will make the memories that much more special.

Make a family tree. You can start with people you remember, your own parents or grandparents, or you can research your family's origins back for generations. A genealogical society should be able to tell you how to do this. You can buy a kit which analyzes your DNA and tells you more about your ancestry.

Make a scrapbook of old family mementos, the program from the third grade spring choir, a ticket stub from a baseball game. Dig out the box where the stuff is stored and go through it. Decide what is meaningful and what can be discarded.

Make a family cookbook, all of the old recipes they've loved over the years: the Christmas cookies, the casseroles, the pies and cakes, and the meatloaf. Copy them into a notebook or onto the computer, or tape the index cards into a scrapbook. Make multiple copies for everyone.

Organize photos. Put them into an album or scan them into the computer so that they can be shared by several people. To the best of your ability, label and date everything. Who is that cute freckled kid?

Load your photos into a digital 8x10 photo frame with a slide show feature to view them in brilliant display one after another.

Get on social media with younger family members. Email or use Facebook, Twitter, or Instagram if they are old enough to use these accounts responsibly. Alternatively have them use mom's account with supervision and assistance.

Traditional crafts. Knitting and crocheting are probably the most popular of the traditional crafts. You can make sweaters, scarves, afghans, stuffed animals, and more. Many of the major yarn companies have websites where you can order patterns, yarns, and supplies (needles, hooks, and other necessities).

People engage in crewel embroidery, needlework, and counted cross-stitch to make pictures and pillow tops.

I have a four-harness floor loom with which I make scarves, placemats, and throw rugs. My daughter-in-law makes beaded jewelry. My aunt tatted lace and crocheted doll clothes.

For centuries both men and women have been creating items for the home and items of beauty. At one time virtually all pots and baking vessels were thrown on a potter's wheel. Beds were covered in homemade quilts in traditional patterns or bold new designs.

I once gathered the stumps of various lengths of lavender and pink advent candles that had accumulated over the years. I melted them down by color and poured the wax (three purple, one pink) into four toilet paper rolls (sealed at the bottom) and inserted purchased wicking to make a new set of advent candles.

If your library uses the Dewey Decimal System, check the spines of books for those numbered 740-750. You will find instructions and ideas for all of the crafts mentioned above and more besides: origami, carving a block of wood, a bar of soap, a rock, or tie dye. You can buy kits with multiple dyes included.

Books on photography begin at 770. If you go out, you can photograph vistas from your walk.

At home you can experiment with still life pictures. Set up an assortment of apples and oranges on a blue placemat. Photograph it from different angles and with different light sources. Try a haphazardly arranged stack of books or pile of shoes.

Take a picture of anyone who comes in your door—standing, sitting, posed or natural, a close-up of the face full on or profile. Ask them to give you smiles and somber looks and a great big grin. Learn to capture the essence of a person. Upload the picture to them or give them a copy.

Draw and paint. If you would rather create your own images instead of photographs, visit an art store or shop online. Procure charcoal or pastels for drawing, acrylic or oil paints and canvas for painting. Use other materials as well, such as mirror frames. If you are just starting to dabble, consider taking lessons at a community college, local art school, or library. Make your own rules.

Magazines at supermarket check-outs have ideas for a new craft project that will take an afternoon or two, especially for Christmas. Create handmade cards or ornaments to give to special people.

Google "crafts." Enter "crafts" on Amazon's search bar to find kits, books, and supplies you can order delivered.

Collecting. When deciding what to collect, consider size, availability, and whether an investment is required. When you are out on your walk, pick up small rocks. Learn to identify them with the help of a field guide with pictures. If near the coast, collect seashells.

If you travel, stop at gift shops for touristy items like thimbles or small spoons. Buy representative postcards and write the year on them. Add to your collection with postcards you receive from friends. Sometimes you can get patches to turn a denim jacket into your personal travel history.

When at home you can collect ticket stubs, vinyl records, books, beer cans, prayer cards. You can collect articles or stories from magazines. Anything that attracts your eye can be collected. Every now and then visit or share your collection. Clean out the superfluous and make room for more.

Fun. Work a jigsaw puzzle, make paper airplanes, blow bubbles, teach yourself a card trick that you can show others. Learn to juggle. Learn to laugh.

Plant an indoor garden or terrarium in a fish tank. Plant an herb garden and snip off the produce to add to salads and meals.

Keep up with your favorite sports team by watching the games and reading what is written about them— who got traded, who is on the injured list, who is in a slump. Look into joining a fantasy sports league.

Make a cardboard castle or a gingerbread house. Make furniture out of poster board. Make moon sand by combining 8 cups of flour with 1 cup of baby oil.

Self-maintenance. Don't forget to take care of yourself. Make bubble bath from ½ cup liquid hand or body soap, 1 Tbsp. sugar, and 1 egg white. Pour it under running water.

Give yourself a manicure or a pedicure. Pick a new color.

Attend to a will or trust to save your heirs headaches when you pass on. Also do an Advance Directive to list your preferences during hospitalizations should you become incapacitated. This is appropriate for any hospital stays (medication preferences, doctors you want on your case) as well as end-of-life decisions. You can find information about any of these documents online, or you can have an attorney draw one up for a simple flat fee.

If you find yourself dragging by mid-afternoon, take a nap, no longer than an hour so that you don't disturb your night sleep patterns.

Do chair exercises, rotating your neck, your shoulders, your arms. Lift your feet to march in place. Get a squeeze ball to exercise your hands to fight off the stiffness.

Do a maintenance walk-through of your home. What is out of place? Worse yet, what doesn't have a place, got dropped down and worked around since it arrived? What is spilling out of its place—books, dishes, magazines? Get someone to help you rearrange the furniture for a new look.

Are there light bulbs that need changing? Does the carpet need cleaning? Arrange for whatever upkeep is needed.

And the closet. Oh, the closet. Pull out what you haven't worn in a while, what you are tired of, what doesn't fit, what you never liked to begin with (that green sweater from Aunt Peggy). Give it to Goodwill which sells it or a homeless shelter which gives it away or a charitable foundation like Red Cross which distributes it in times of emergency such as flood or fire. Whatever you do, the odds are that your donation will somehow find a woman who looks good in green.

Kitchen. A lot of pleasant time can be spent in the kitchen. Make a pot of soup or a super salad with whatever is on hand. Dust out the casserole dish and make yourself a nice meal instead of microwave defrost. Fix a fancy dessert.

Bake cookies or a homemade bread. Give them to a friend or take them to the fire department.

Squeeze fresh lemonade. Eat a popsicle. Make a special trip to the kitchen just to pour and savor a glass of ice water.

Random acts of kindness. Surprise someone with a small act of kindness. Take note of that person, either a stranger or someone you see frequently. Assess their possible needs or wants. The most basic need is to be recognized as a person. You can fill that need with some small act that says "this is for you."

For instance, nod and say hello to a person you pass on the sidewalk or in the corridor. With someone on the elevator, go further and comment on the weather. These small exchanges boost both their mood and yours.

Hold the door for either gender regardless of your gender. We are no longer dealing with twelve-foot-tall oak doors on a medieval cathedral.

Write a note of appreciation to someone for their presence, or a note of kindness or compassion. Hand it to the person directly or put it where they will find it. My grandson's first-grade class wrote anonymous notes and placed them in each others' backpacks.

Give a small gift of a candy bar, a single carnation, a cross-stitch mini. Give something you buy inexpensively or create. Don't overdo or you'll make the person uncomfortable.

Let someone in front of you at the checkout. If someone with a few items faces a long line, or if someone with a fussy infant approaches, gesture for her to step in front of you.

Send a card or prepare food for the bereaved. Check in on them from time to time. Invite them over regularly.

Follow the simple methodology. See the person. See what small act of kindness you can do for the person. Then do it without fuss. For that moment you are connected with that person. Both are less lonely.

Challenge for Change. Do an act of kindness for someone.

8. Getting Out

Congratulations!
Today is your day.
You're off to Great Places!
You're off and away!
Dr. Seuss, *Oh, the Places You'll Go!*

Elevator problems. Since October 2018 elevator A of my senior apartment building had been nonworking. When elevator B stopped working on a Thursday in May 2019, I and eighty other residents were stuck. The first floor of the building was commercial while the apartments were on the upper two floors.

Some people who used canes or walked on their own ventured the twenty-one stairs. I could make it up or down a step at a time with both hands on the rail, but I couldn't carry my walker. Without that I was immobilized once I reached the ground floor. I had to stay in.

On Friday they told us that the elevator wouldn't be fixed until Tuesday, the day after Memorial Day. In other words, they were unwilling to pay the overtime to have someone come in on the holiday weekend.

Tuesday became Wednesday, and Wednesday became Thursday when about thirty residents met in the activity room, gathered by one ninety-two-year-old resident who had sent around flyers. A reporter from the local CBS affiliate interviewed people to find out the impact of a week without an elevator. She tried to interview the property owner, who had an office downtown, but he was always unavailable. The report aired on the local newscast.

I was restricted to my floor, mostly to my apartment. I knew people in the building but had never been to their apartments and didn't know where they lived. The grocery delivery persons shlepped up and down the stairs. People missed appointments.

At first I lived day-to-day with no problem. I usually went out only four or five days a week anyhow. As time went on, I became different, quieter internally. I didn't particularly care to go out. I spent more time sitting, even lying down, less time doing. I was showing the early signs of depression.

On Saturday evening—Day 10—my son and his wife visited. They tackled the stairs with take-out Chinese. As we ate, the property manager informed us that elevator B had been fixed.

I had been roused from my inward focus by their visit. After they left I took the elevator down. Even though it was dusk, I sat on the bench in front of the building and watched the pedestrian traffic go by. I was out. On Sunday I walked down to the farmers' market.

After staying in for so long, it would have been just as easy to stay in forever. I was attuned to it, had lowered my expectations of the world. I was becoming depressed and was tempted to sink down into it.

Getting out fires up the brain. If at all possible, even a bench in front of the building, you need that stimulus. In this chapter I have provided many suggestions for places to go, and I am sure you can come up with more.

Six months later elevator A has undergone a complete overhaul and is now working. Elevator B is down for a similar overhaul and is worked on every Wednesday when the moon is full and the creek don't rise. The building owner is facing criminal charges and has been in court several times. Meanwhile several residents have filed civil suits against him.

Transportation. First we have to get you out. If you drive a car, you are extremely fortunate. Enhance your chances of being able to continue to drive by taking a refresher course in driving for seniors offered by AARP and other organizations. You may find you prefer to drive during the day or on surface streets.

If you don't drive, learn your way around on the bus system. Call and ask for schedules for the routes that run by your home, or look them up online.

If you have a smart phone, get the app to sign up for Lyft and Uber. Once you are registered online with a payment method, you can use your cell phone to request a ride from your present location, such as home, to a new destination. A private taxi is more expensive, but you should keep their number handy just in case.

If you are disabled, the bus company or local government probably offers a taxi or van service. In many localities it is called Access (paratransit). You must register with them in advance. You make an appointment ahead of your scheduled ride. The fee is modest. Be sure to let them know if you are using a walker or a wheelchair.

Remind friends and family that you need to get out. Have a specific location to suggest, or tag along on their errands. If they take you to Target, have a list of three or four items. Don't insist on wandering the whole store.

If you live in a structured residence, they probably have a van. They may use it for group outings, but they may also use it to help people with individual appointments.

Whatever your means of transportation, getting out is more of a hassle than it used to be. Don't give in to ennui. Don't tell yourself that it is easier to stay home. It is, but you will benefit from the effort to get out, to make it part of your rhythm. Oh, the places you'll go! Enjoy them. Getting new perspectives will make your four walls seem less confining.

Walking. We've already discussed walking--up and down the block, to the park, to the store. If you come across someone else who walks, ask if they would like to walk with you. If you have a caregiver, she is being paid to walk with you if you desire. Look into walking tours of Europe and other countries.

Some city parks have playground equipment where you can watch the kids swing and slide. A few have skate parks where kids and adults practice their ollies and flips.

Hiking. Go to a city, county, or state park with several undeveloped acres. Often you can follow trails marked by blazes on trees. The trails may be rated by degree of difficulty, from a simple slope through the woods to a washed-out gulley piled with broken boulders. Look for local meet-up groups of hikers online. I once picked up a hiking guide from a nature center which listed all of the trails in the county with location, length, and degree of difficulty.

Other natural sites. Every locale has vistas of interest, from the mountains of Colorado to the canyon of Arizona to the corn of Kansas or the colors of New England. The Badlands present a desert landscape. Seek out the beauty around you.

Historic cemetery. Visit a local cemetery and read the tombstones. Many cemeteries are at least one hundred years old. Tombstones have changed in that time. Previously they had more embellishments or thoughts engraved on them. Note the clusters of family members, the dates of birth and death, the longevity. Sadly there were more baby and child markers back then.

Bus tours. Several companies offer bus tours through specific areas of the country such as the Mississippi River Valley. Lasting anywhere from a few days to a week or more, the price includes lodging, some meals, and a tour guide to fill you in on all the points of interest. You can get bus tours of Europe and other countries as well. Check with your local travel agent or online.

To find out about getting a passport, check with your post office or look online. Even if you don't intend to travel abroad, a passport can be useful for checking in for domestic flights.

Cruises. While you're talking to the travel agent, ask about cruises. If there is water—inland or ocean—a cruise ship plies those waters. Known for their cuisine, entertainment, and amenities, cruise ships typically stop at new ports each day for you to explore and shop. Price the tours before you sign up for them.

Again a travel agent can help identify cruises especially for seniors at special prices. Some ships are inappropriate for people with mobility issues because they have a lot of walking and stairs. Also cabins with handicap amenities are available.

Water. Water has mystical properties. We evolved from sea creatures, and we are on average 60% water. It calls to us to reflect, to look into ourselves. It represents the topic for lyric poetry and the remembrances of historic crossings and naval battles and settlements.

At Eden Park in Cincinnati one can look across the Ohio River, muddy and swollen from the spring rains, to the red-roofed houses on the Kentucky side. At one time Kentucky was a slave state while Ohio was free, and the

river represented the boundary between slavery and freedom.

Walden Pond is dinky, a pool of moss-green water
surrounded by woods, yet it was the inspiration for Henry
David Thoreau's classic of the same name. It had a cabin
but no picnic tables, and my husband, the three kids, and
I sat on a blanket for our picnic. After lunch we walked
around the pond in less than an hour.

Food. Everybody's favorite destination. Eat out
inexpensively at a fast food or diner. Each week pick a
different one to see who has the best burgers (or veggie
burgers). Eat in. Bring a magazine or newspaper, or people-watch. Sit by the window or outside.

Go to a deli where they list the sandwiches on a
board behind the counter, and they wrap their creations in
white paper. Be sure to get a side of fresh slaw.

Visit a neighborhood bar or pub. They often have
excellent pub grub. Sit at the bar, chat with the bartender
and the person next to you, and watch the sporting event
on the big screen.

Try other cuisines in town. Typically every ethnicity is represented—Italian, Korean, Greek, Russian,
French, Chinese—in addition to American from different
parts of the country--Southwest, New England, deep
South. Invite an acquaintance to meet you there. Make
sure there's an understanding if you expect each to pick
up their own tab.

Explore the grocery rather than just breezing in
and out to pick up the coffee on aisle six and the celery in
produce. Look item by item. What other delicacies can be
found in aisle six? How many kinds of mushrooms are
there in produce? The freezer has everything from cocktail shrimp to blueberry pie.

Self-care. Get a haircut, a massage, a manicure. Let somebody fuss over you. Chat with the person who is supplying the service. Tell them about your grandchildren.

Shopping. Especially in inclement weather, stores are a likely destination whether you have purchases to make or not. You may need help with the grocery shopping every week or two. Smaller errands are more manageable: drugstore, clothing stores, big box store, hardware, crafts, toys, books.

Browse furniture stores even if you have no needs. Check out a store with vintage clothing or costumes, a consignment shop, a thrift shop, a pawnshop, a secondhand store.

Poke into restaurant supply, art supply, auto supply, lighting supply. As you drive or ride from one store to another, be on the lookout for something new to explore. Check the ads in the hometown tabloid.

Do not be afraid to say, "Just looking." If all you are seeking is an afternoon's amusement, don't be intimidated into buying something you don't need. If you can't leave a store without making a purchase, go to a museum instead.

Museums. You can find museums everywhere, and everything and everyone has a museum devoted to them. Major metropolitan areas have museums of art, history, natural history, science, and children's museums.

North Andover MA has a weaving museum. A refrigeration research museum is in Brighton MI. Clay pots can be found in the Smithsonian, the Tucson Museum, or the Victoria and Albert Museum. Google something you want to see along with the word "museum," and you will find its location.

If you are in a particular area and want to know what museums are at hand, Google "museums" and the city, state. I tried Billings MT and found a list of ten museums.

Look for Presidential libraries and also birthplaces and workplaces of famous people such as authors. The Ernest Hemingway Home and Museum where he often worked is in Key West FL, while the museum of his birthplace is in Oak Park IL.

All major sports have Halls of Fame. Baseball is in Cooperstown NY. Football is in Canton OH. For hoops, you can find the Basketball Hall of Fame in Springfield MA. Although not exactly a sport, the Rock and Roll Hall of Fame is in Cleveland OH.

Sports. Speaking of sporting events, is there a major league team near you—baseball, football, basketball, hockey, or soccer? Most of the sports have minor league teams sprinkled across the country. The Dayton Dragons, the Reds AAA affiliate, are sold out almost every night. Minor league teams are usually in a more intimate venue and are less expensive.

Visit a racetrack. Pick a horse with an interesting name. Check the odds. Bet on it if you like, or just cheer for it as it comes around the stretch.

Casinos. If you are able to walk away from the table when your budgeted gambling nest egg has been exhausted, visit a casino. They also offer quality entertainment and lavish buffets. Some casinos run a free bus from the city to the casino.

For lower stakes gambling, check out weekly bingo games at senior centers and churches. My aunt won the air fare to come to my sister's wedding at a church bingo game.

Library. Scan the numbers at the end of the book-shelves in nonfiction. Often these are arranged by the Dewey Decimal System. For example the numbering starts with 000 (computer science, information, and general works) and passes through 300 (social sciences) all the way through to 700 (arts and recreation).

Pick a topic to investigate further and look at those books on the shelves. Choose a book and take it to the nearest chair to browse. After perusing it, set it aside to check out later or leave it to be reshelved, and pick another book from another shelf.

For fiction, keep a list of authors to try out. Ask people who they read, and pay attention to reviews in magazines. Consult the web for lists of best books like 100 from www.abebooks.com.

If you are browsing fiction in the library with no clue, look into the authors who have a lot of books on the shelf. They are popular for a reason. I found Clive Cussler that way.

Places where people gather. While at the library, ask about upcoming events and groups that gather there. Around town also ask about writing groups, church groups, nonprofit organizations, political parties, garden clubs, and senior centers. Perhaps there is an astronomy club or a local history club. Look for a local weekly tabloid (often set out at restaurants and other places for free), and read all of the columns and ads with a red pen in hand to mark gathering places that you find.

My community has separate societies for begonias, African violets, and orchids. Several bridge groups play weekly. A nonprofit organization is soliciting members.

Look at the website for your local city or county government. Google the words "city" or "county" with the name and state. They will have a list of governmental meetings and perhaps meetings of organizations as well. Better yet, call them and ask what goes on in town. If the website has a menu at the top, look especially for "visitors."

Every city has its interesting tidbits. Colonel Sanders (KFC), Dave Thomas (Wendy's), and Tom Forkner (Waffle House) all lived in Oak Ridge TN during WWII. Oak Ridge is known as the "Secret City" because its location was not given out during the atomic bomb project.

Educational opportunities. Community colleges sometimes have special deals for seniors. They offer a potpourri of classes from college prep to trade to personal interest. They usually have classes on Saturdays as well as evenings.

I randomly selected Nassau Community College on Long Island NY (www.ncc.edu). Its catalog lists the full range of classes one would expect for freshmen and sophomores in college. Its listings for the letter "I" are Inner Global Studies, Italian, Interior Design, Information Technology—quite the range. For credit classes there is a senior observer program. Persons 60+ may attend a class without receiving credit on a space-available basis.

The school also has a full range of noncredit lifelong learning classes offering certificate programs and teaching business skills, real estate, and self-improvement for example

Other community colleges offer trades. In most locales people can access a community college on its own campus with classroom buildings administration buildings, a student center, and sporting facilities.

Four-year colleges and universities also often allow seniors to take or audit unclaimed spaces in classes for free or at reduced cost. Check with the admissions office. Also look into their sporting programs. Spend an afternoon watching the Crimson Tide.

Get out. You will not fall off the edge of the world. Columbus already proved that. If you exercise ordinary caution, you will not likely get into a situation that you can't get out of. Sometimes we behave as though we have imaginary leashes on ourselves. I can go this far, but no further. Challenge those limits, and extend your comfort zone. If you find you cannot move out further, then explore in depth what is around you. Try to see something new each day, even if it is from the same vantage point as the bench you sat in yesterday.

Challenge for Change. Find a museum or dedicated site in your town that you had not known about.

9. Volunteer and Part-Time Positions

Wheresoever you go, go with all your heart.
Confucius

Commitment. Activities at Home (Chapter 7) and Getting Out (Chapter 8) you do at your own pace. You do it maybe today, maybe tomorrow, maybe sometime else instead. You set your own schedule. Volunteer activities and employment differ in that you commit to be in a certain place at a certain time. Limited at-home activities exist, but you still promise to do them within a specific time frame.

Either way, you are giving of yourself to someone or something, with or without pay. Look at your present schedule, and decide how many hours/week you want to commit to such an effort. Do something you love.

Common volunteer opportunities. The following are examples of places often looking for people:
   o Churches (office, outreach, church carnival)
   o Schools (room parent, PTA, book fair)
   o Hospitals (transport, reception, gift shop)
   o Nursing facilities (bingo, visiting, reading aloud)
   o Libraries (reshelving, tutoring, organizing groups)
   o Youth activities (sports, Scouts)
   o Civic organizations (Kiwanis, Lions, Soroptimists)
   o National/international organizations (Red Cross, Salvation Army, Amnesty International)
   o Crisis lines (suicide, other, training provided)
   You may need screening or training, especially to work with kids.

During an eclectic volunteering lifetime, I have run a book fair and a flea market, played cards at a homeless day care program, served as a room mom, kept the books as the state treasurer for a national women's organization, served meals at Thanksgiving dinners, produced a monthly newsletter and played couples bridge for a local organization, stood on street corners with signs supporting the mental health levy, attended more committee meetings than I care to remember including Parish Council, lectored, and taught CCD as it was known then. For much of this time, I balanced this with a husband and three kids. I loved the involvement and connecting with people. Presently I address and mail envelopes to lapsed and new members of a local organization.

Web volunteering opportunities. A comprehensive website for volunteer opportunities is VolunteerMatch.org. Enter your areas of interest or your skill category and your zip code. A list giving brief summaries of local opportunities will open. As you scan down the list, you can check places of interest to get a more detailed account of the opening along with desired skills. You can inquire directly, often just by clicking on a space.

The AARP website Connect2Affect.org has information about volunteering and takes you back to VolunteeerMatch.org

If you give your email address, you will sometimes receive an email with new volunteer opportunities in your community. Below are opportunities I found in my mailbox one day:

o serve on board for organization that saves and sanitizes hotel soap for the developing world
o rescue cats at risk for euthanasia

- o find social services and housing for entertainment professionals in need
- o be program assistant for senior center
- o propagate plants for nature center
- o speak on panel in health and medical fields for careers program for afterschool
- o play merchant in a "mock city" to encourage students in good financial decisions
- o collect produce boxes and weigh for hunger-relief agencies.

As you can see, there is a wide variety from one-time to ongoing commitment, helping the developing world and animals and social services for different groups. If you can imagine it, then it is happening somewhere, and the websites will help you to imagine it.

Testimonial. My friend Mary writes:

> As a child I learned to give back from my mother. It started when I was ten years old and she arranged for me to be a teacher's helper for the kinder class at Vacation Bible School. As a teenager I served meals to Seniors at church luncheons. The habit serves me well, even as I have become a Senior myself. My mother delivered Meals on Wheels when she was in her 70s, and many of her clients were younger than she was.
>
> My most recent volunteer activity involved 80 hours of training to become a CASA – Court Appointed Special Advocate. I am now a sworn officer of the Court and have a foster child assigned to me. My role is to develop a relationship with the child and advocate for her in dependency court as Social Services works to find an adoption placement for her. Giving back keeps me active,

engaged with the world, and thankful for the goodness in my own life.

Compassion. Who are these people who need your help? The poor, the hungry, the old, the young, the sick, the unlearned, the marginalized, those who have a void with no way to fill it but for the help of volunteers. In other words, society won't pay to help them but they won't go away. Add the forests and the animals and the climate.

As learned in the chapter on self-esteem, the worth of these people is equivalent to yours or anyone else's. They need your compassion ("I feel for you") not your pity ("You poor thing"). It would be a mistake to talk down to them. They have much to teach you about forbearance, courage, and life itself, and possibly also quantum mechanics. Listen to them.

Part-time work. Volunteer positions can be as little as 3-4 hours/week or a fulltime commitment. Part-time work often requires around 20 hours/week, sometimes including evenings and weekends.

The difference of course is that one gets paid for part-time work but not for volunteering. The rewards can be worthwhile in either capacity. If you work for pay, report it to Social Security at 800-772-1213 or www.ssa.gov. Generally speaking, when you reach full retirement age your earnings no longer reduce your benefits.

A part-time job usually has higher expectations than a volunteer position. Attendance requirements are stricter. The dress code may be better defined. The work ethic may expect more. Those big bucks don't come cheap. Are you seeking to be in an office or out in the field? Some positions require a car.

Websites. Two popular employment websites are Indeed.com and LinkedIn.com. You can browse Indeed.com relatively easily. I didn't find a way to access LinkedIn.com without joining and giving my contact information. Since I wasn't actually interested in getting a job, I didn't care to be contacted. They were extolled in a webinar on part-time employment that I attended.

Experiment. Deciding to see what was out there, I entered "part-time help wanted" and the name of a typical Midwestern city on the search engine. From the responses that showed up, I picked one that was specifically part-time. A number of job titles showed up with a brief description of each position. The job titles included:

- o retail, by far the most plentiful field. Typical were sales associates (cash registers and stocking shelves, able to lift up to fifty pounds), assistant managers, photographers for the photo sales, retail specialists who visit stores to make sure a company's product is in stock
- o health fields, including RNs, home health aides, adult day care workers
- o dock/warehouse worker, fulfilling orders
- o call center, administrative assistant

Qualifications are listed (usually high school or four-year college any degree), number of hours, and sometimes salaries. Each site tells you how to apply further, usually by filling out a form with basic information.

Scam alert. I offer websites that appear to be safe, but I can't guarantee anything. If you look them up, it is at your own risk.

I came across one site that asked only for name, email address, and date of birth (mm/dd/yyyy). That set up a red flag. Usually such detailed information is not requested until later in the hiring process. With a name and date of birth, my health records can be requested over the phone. Also do not give out social security number or bank account information until you have established whom you are doing business with.

As an added precaution, you can verify the recipient of information when you are further along in the hiring process. Suppose you are offered a job by the Snuffen Co. in Boulder, CO. Go to the Snuffen Co. website and tell them that you want to verify an employment offer. See if the name/phone you have been given matches up with their company records. Caller ID can be manipulated to make it look like the call is coming from a legitimate source when in fact it is an impostor.

Stay away from the website that asks you to send a "modest" amount of money to cover training manuals or other materials. Once they have you, they will require more money to continue. You are faced with a choice of whether to send good money after bad, or to back out and lose your initial investment. All the while the website hypes how successful you will be and how much money you will make. Some people, and in particular seniors, have lost sums of money this way. The simple rule of thumb is don't send money. Other opportunities don't require it.

Résumé. A potential employer may ask you to submit a résumé. You should draw one up in preparation. Generally it is no more than two pages; emphasize what you have to offer, in particular your past experience.

Assess your skills and experience. Think not only of previous jobs but also life experiences in working with teens, seniors, veterans, or some other special group. Looking after Aunt May when she had Alzheimer's counts as valuable experience. So does running the flea market for the PTA. What were your "additional duties as assigned" in your prior work history? Being able to inventory and order office supplies is a bonus. Include relevant related activities, such as church treasurer or volunteer with a mental health program. You can get advice on the web on different styles of résumés.

Consider multiple résumés emphasizing different skill sets for different types of position desired. Résumés can even be useful in applying for volunteer work.

Finding the right position---volunteer or part-time--may take time. To the extent possible, network. Let people at church or the senior center know you are looking. They may hear of something.

Don't wait to be asked to fill a position. If you see a place where you would like to try to fit in, ask if they have any openings. Bring a résumé that they can keep on file.

Age discrimination. The Age Discrimination in Employment Act of 1967 (ADEA) protects certain applicants and employees 40 years of age and older from discrimination on the basis of age in hiring, promotion, discharge, compensation, or terms, conditions or privileges of employment.

The ADEA is enforced by the Equal Employment Opportunity Commission (EEOC), which is split into fifteen districts. You can find your district on the map at www.eeoc.gov. Call for more information at 202-663-4900 (TTY) 202-663-4494.

Challenge for Change. Make a broad list of your skills, from child care to accounting to closet-organizing. Look for patterns and possible uses for these skills. If it's closet-organizing, then apply to a homeless shelter which receives clothing donations or a consignment shop.

10. Living with Less

The rules are different now, and we often see it in older folks' freedom to give things away. Hoarding, possessing, collecting, and impressing others with their things, their house, or their travels are of less and less interest to them. Inner brightness, still holding life's sadness and joy, is its own reward, its own satisfaction, and their best and truest gift to the world.
Richard Rohr, *Falling Upwards.*

Practical matters. We have to consider many practical matters when we live alone. We may have to change our residence, and the amount of property we can take with us may be reduced.

The effects of stress have to be considered. Are we taking care of ourselves? Planning for and preparing meals for one person is tricky. Holidays and fear of being alone present a challenge.

Who will take care of us when we are sick? These and other matters need to be thought out when we face life alone. On the other hand, many call these the golden years, a time of fewer responsibilities, more leisure, the satisfaction of seeing our projects (including our kids) come to fruition.

Downsizing. When you move to a new living space, most likely it is smaller, as house to apartment to assisted living and on it goes. You never have enough room for all the things you want to keep—Grandma's picture, a carved wooden sailboat from the Mediterranean cruise, a square glass bottle with a cork stopper to hold paper clips, a plaster Peter Rabbit that your son painted one Easter, and the list goes on. Three bookcases hold fiction, nonfiction, and finds from Half-Price Books. You have two sets of pots and pans and three sets of dishes.

If you have significant property including furniture, you can Google estate sales or yard sales to find a company which for a fee will arrange to have it all sold. Otherwise you can box it up and hope you can find somebody to take it to Goodwill. Generally such stores don't pick up unless large items are involved. Consider also junk removal services. Some of them recycle usable stuff.

In the hutch you discover eleven tablecloths. They evoke so many memories, of Christmas, Thanksgiving, a housewarming, buffets. How can you part with the memories? You could possibly give one or two to the kids, but they have their own traditions now.

A tablecloth is just that, a piece of cloth that covered the table. The people around the table were what made the occasion memorable. You remember your parents, now gone, who reversed the role of host and guest once your family was established. You remember the single sister now living in Chicago who relished the role of aunt. And you remember the kids in their various stages of growth who guaranteed a spill of milk or gravy or cranberry sauce onto the tablecloth. You didn't consider the tablecloth sacred then but mopped the spill up as best you could and soaked the tablecloth the next day in the laundry tub. The child was forgiven.

The question is, will you be any more or less lonely for having eleven tablecloths? Will it make you happier to surround yourself by all eleven as a reminder of what has been? That may be good for an evening of nostalgia now and then, but that gets old too. You have entered a new phase of life. The memories are important. The things that tie you to those memories are not.

It was the people who were important. Therefore in your evening of reminiscing you need to reach out to the people, not pieces of fabric. You can telephone the sister in Chicago and recall past times. Or you can e-mail the kids and remind them of the snapping of the wishbone.

You set the tablecloths aside and move on to the chest containing the silverware, twelve place settings used at most three or four times a year. Polishing the silver in advance was part of the ritual of the holiday. Nobody wants the silver set either, but it is too valuable to give away. You will have to find someplace to sell it. So many decisions. So much to do.

If the family is supportive, you can walk away with only what you need and let them decide what to do with the stuff. It's best not to watch it go. Note that they can only do this with your consent. Legally it is still your property, and nobody can remove it without your permission. If it happens that it gets left behind when the house is sold, then it is forfeit.

Better to deal with it while you can. Now you can enjoy the clean feeling of being less burdened by possessions. Being surrounded by material reminders of the past only makes you feel lonelier. You have entered that phase of your life in which you are letting go of the things.

Selling the house. The House Whisperer says a home is two things: the structure and the story. The structure includes the walls and the fixtures that protect you from the elements and make the house livable. Beyond that is the story of your family that the dwelling tells, from the flooring and the furniture to the pictures on the walls and the knickknack on the bathroom vanity. Your visitors enter into this story.

In downsizing you have removed much of the excess clutter. In preparing the home to sell, you want to take out your story that made it home. Buyers are looking to make it their home, and they need to be able to imagine their own story superimposed on the dwelling.

The option of moving out before the house is sold is possible, but it is difficult to sell on altogether empty home. Talk to your realtor if you have one.

You can sell by owner, but you have to know what to do in terms of listing, showing, and paperwork. You have to be prepared to deal with the bank and local or county government. Above all you have to be prepared for the closing to make sure that title is transferred properly. A multitude of papers gets signed at the closing.

If you decide to get a realtor, do not select Cousin Ned who does it as a hobby. Pick someone whose livelihood depends on how well they sell real estate. Consult the reviews of the realtor's former clients online. It should be someone you personally get along with, someone you trust to show your home affably. Read the contract and find out for how long the agreement is in force. You can change realtors if the house doesn't sell in the time of the contract. These same principles hold for condominiums.

The house is twice as lonely once that sign goes up in the yard. If you don't hear from the realtor concerning showings, contact her frequently. Close off unused rooms. Keep the house ready for showing at all times—clutter picked up, beds made, no dishes in the sink.

Keep busy by doing changes of address for subscriptions, utilities, other correspondents. Go out and pick up some real stationery. One or two a day write letters to family and friends from your Christmas card list telling them of your move, adding personal touches about your hopes and dreams for your new location. An alternate is to do a group email. Give everyone your new address.

Talk to your neighbors one-by-one, again talking about the good you expect to come of this. Keep your sense of humor; joke about the process. To your very closest neighbor you can admit your fears and your pain. Tell your neighbors you expect them to take care of the buyer, thus sowing a seed for new relationships. If moving locally, invite them to visit.

Keep hold of yourself by touching base with others. By telling them that it will be okay, you will soon start to believe it.

Challenge for Change. Live in the moment. What do you need to be doing right now? Anything else that needs to be done is not pertinent for now. Perhaps you need to be sorting bookshelves. On the other hand, perhaps you need to take an interesting book you came across and sit down with it without guilt. Live in the moment.

11. Independent Living

Louisa was slow and still in her movements; it took her a long time to prepare her tea; but when ready it was set forth with as much grace as if she had been a veritable guest to her own self. The little square table stood exactly in the centre of the kitchen, and was covered with a starched linen cloth whose border pattern of flowers glittered. Louisa had a damask napkin on her tea-tray, where were arranged a cut-glass tumbler full of teaspoons, a silver cream-pitcher, a china sugar-bowl, and one pink china cup and saucer.

Mary Wilkins Freeman, "A New England Nun," *A New England Nun and Other Stories,* 1891.

Your own space. Whether you own or rent, living independently means that you control your own space. You determine what goes in the refrigerator, and you raid it at any time. You set the thermostat, and you pay the energy bill. When to close the curtains at night and when to open them in the morning is up to you.

You make your own rules and bend them when you need to. No staff hovers to tell you when to go to bed or to ask you if you have had a bowel movement.

Over a quarter of all people over the age of 65 live independently, and the trend is growing. . You wanted to maintain your independent lifestyle in your own home, sometimes with the support of family and caregivers. "Most older people who live alone express a keen desire to maintain their independence." [Kaplan et al.]

You may still live in the house where your children were raised, where you lived with a spouse, where you now live alone, or you may have moved to a newer townhouse. Either of these has property which must be maintained, with perhaps the solace of a garden where you plant zinnias on the sunny side and impatiens on the shady side. Other fancier types of housing exist which are distinguished mainly by the cost.

An apartment you lease; a condominium (condo) you own. Either way, your holdings are restricted to the space inside the front door and perhaps a storage locker. It may have as many as two or three or more bedrooms and two baths, or may be a studio efficiency, one large room with waking area and bath. A hallway is lined with neighbors' doors which swing open from time to time.

An accessory dwelling unit (ADU) is a separate apartment or cottage on the grounds of a single family home. Often called "granny units," they support an inter-generational lifestyle. I met a neighbor who told me she was having an ADU built in her daughter's backyard, a small independent house on a slab with living room, bed-room, small kitchen, and bathroom. It would take less than a year to complete and cost $40,000. (Expect cost overruns.) Once there she can live rent-free, responsible for her own maintenance, in proximity to her daughter's family but not on top of them.

Senior living apartments is a term used for a building or complex of independent apartments whose tenancy rule requires that a resident must be a certain age, often over 55. They do not provide services such as cleaning, laundry, or meals. They are often arranged with seniors in mind with elevators and laundry facilities on each floor. They may have an activity room which can be reserved, but often no planned activities. In essence they are independent living for a certain age group. The neighbors are generally quiet, and sometimes the rent is subsidized. Check with local government for availability. For a nationwide call center, call the Eldercare Locator at 800-677-1116.

Some people live in a bedroom of a family member's house. Although not as independent, you can still call your space your own and choose your lifestyle up to the point where it impacts others.

Living with a family member generally does not include living with a spouse. That counts as a couple and has its own chemistry. Living with a family member could be any family member – a sister, a nephew, to name a few. Most commonly we think of living with a son or a daughter and their nuclear family.

Recall the home of Charlie Bucket in *Willy Wonka and the Chocolate Factory*. Both sets of grandparents live in Charlie's house. They are depicted as two couples lying toe-to-toe in a great bed in the living room with a single quilt covering them all. From there they contribute to the conversation of the family, adding comments based on their collective store of wisdom.

Now we call it intergenerational living. It could mean doubling up the grandkids to give grandma her own bedroom. Or sleeping on a futon in the living room, retiring for the night while the rest of the adults in the family watch the late show. Or an RV or ADU in the yard, maybe or maybe not with liberal access to the main house.

When your own kids were little, you were (often with your spouse) the caregivers. Now the roles seem to have reversed. You're not comfortable with it, not adjusted to this. You don't know when to lean, when to stand as erect as you can, when to ask for help, when to try it on your own. Your family members don't know when to intervene. The kids don't know where you fit in or whether to take direction from you. The dynamics are uncertain from the beginning.

A hypothetical example. On the first morning since she moved in with her son's family, Sheila came down for breakfast fully dressed, hair still wet. Ordinarily she would have eaten breakfast in her robe and then showered. But she is living with others now, and she wondered what the custom was.

She noted that her daughter-in-law Melody was wearing a robe. One question answered.

She hesitated. It's not her kitchen. Should she help herself to coffee or sit and wait to be served? Melody asks, "Would you like me to get you a cup of coffee?" She can answer either: "No, I'd like to get my own."

Or: "Yes, that would be lovely."

"Creamer and two sweeteners."

She was making rapid progress. She felt hopeful that they could make this work and looked forward to her new way of life.

She had many more questions to resolve. They haven't discussed finances. She felt she should be paying rent and contributing to the groceries. What about her medical appointments? How to schedule them so that someone can drive her?

Either families talk these things out, or there is frustration in the relationship. Try to love; try to give. In some families the siblings take turns hosting mom or dad so that it is less of a burden. In most families mom or dad is considered as a member of the family so they fit right in, with occasional frictions of course but not constant tension.

Daytime. When family members are at work or at school during the day, you may find yourself alone. What are the ground rules? Sometimes family members discourage you from going out for walk by yourself. In cases where you have some mental confusion, the fear is that you will be unable to find your way home. In some cases this is very real. Or it may be over-protection, but you have to ask yourself if you are willing to abide by their ground rules.

I knew a woman who complained in group because her family said she was not supposed to go out on her own for a walk. People were willing to take her. I could see the family's concern, because she often was unable to find her way from the break room to the group room without confusion.

One option is for your family to speak to the neighbors that they know best. They can invite some neighbors over to visit you on an occasional basis. And you have the other skills for defeating loneliness set out in this book.

Elder abuse. A word of caution: In rare instances, living with family can lead to situations of elder abuse, when you are harmed physically, emotionally, or financially. You can report elder abuse to Adult Protective Services at 800-222-8000.

Independent living with assistance. The amount of assistance you require depends largely on the Activities of Daily Living (ADLs) or Instrumental Activities of Daily Living (IADLs). These two scales, used by social workers and others involved in planning care, list the minimum amount of maintenance needed to cope each day. Some scales vary slightly from one resource to another, but in essence they are as follows:

Activities of Daily Living (ADLs).
- Motion: can change positions and walk inde-pendently
- Feeding: can feed self
- Dressing: can select and put on seasonally proper clothing
- Personal hygiene: can bathe and can manage oral, nail, and hair care
- Continence management: mental and physical ability to properly use the bathroom or inconti-nence aids

Instrumental Activities of Daily Living (IADLs).
- Managing mail and bills
- Managing finances and investments
- Managing appointments and transportation
- Shopping and meal prep
- House cleaning and home maintenance
- Managing communications (phone and online)
- Managing medications

When you are unable to perform one of more of these activities, then you ask for assistance usually from family or an agency caregiver. Sometimes you need only a little help such as a reminder or someone standing by, but in cases of full dependency, you need others to do the task.

Home care aides and home health aides are two different types of assistance givers. Home care aides can do any of the tasks on the ADL and IADL lists other than medication management. They can remind you to take meds but not actually administer them. Be clear about what tasks you need help with.

If you have too much time alone, an aide can be hired solely for the sake of companionship. This means spending actual interaction time with you. It does not include watching television together. The aide can take you out for walks, drives, errands, or outings. You can sit and converse, or play cards together, or bake cookies, or go through a closet at your request.

A home care aide may have received training from an agency, but she does not need to be licensed or certified. She may be from an agency or may work independently. In that case, there is no background check. You have to be careful about whom you hire. In 2018 the national average charged by home health agencies was $20.50 per hour according to the website www.payingforseniorcare.org. Medicare does not pay for non-medical services.

Home health aides can be nurses, social workers, occupational or physical therapists, nurse's aides, or other medical professionals. They provide a higher level of skilled nursing care such as checking vital signs or assisting with medications and medical equipment. The average cost for a home health care visit is $135, with the possibility that Medicare and other resources will cover at least some.

In order to get the expense covered, your doctor must note the need for medical assistance in your treatment plan and write a referral to the home health agency. You and the agency set up the prescribed visits. The agency then bills Medicare.

The Institute on Aging (SF) reports that 65% of older adults with long-term care needs rely exclusively on family and friends for their support. The care provided by family and friends can determine whether the older person can remain at home. 50% of those with no family caregiver are admitted to a nursing home as opposed to 7% with family caregiver. [www.ioaging.org/aging-in-america]

Shut-in. A special circumstance of living independently would be those who are shut in, who cannot get out on a regular basis to run errands and see friends or go to church. It may have happened gradually, first with not going out in the evening, or not going far from home. Eventually you find yourself shut-in in the sense that you can't go out because of physical limitations and lack of any way to go out. You must make provision to have your needs met such as in assisted living below. Try to arrange to have someone check in with you daily.

Every state is divided into areas, and each has an Area Agency on Aging. The purpose is to serve the needs of older persons such as shut-ins. If you require help, if you have no way to get your needs met, contact your state agency. You can find your local Area Agency by emailing www.n4a.org or calling 202-872-0888.

How will you meet your need for social contact when you don't go out? One way is to use the telephone. Call every third cousin on a regular basis. Be upbeat, friendly, and brief so that they look forward to your calls.

Initiate conversations with every person who stops by, the visiting nurse who takes your blood pressure or the person who brings your Meals on Wheels. Show an interest in the person. Again these will most likely be brief, but they will give some feeling of satisfaction to your need for social contacts.

If you don't have one, consider getting a computer. Some computers are designed for non-geeks with more simplified access to email, text, and the web. This will help you research home health care agencies, meals on wheels programs, or other services. You can also look up the standings for any professional sport, find a web page on any famous (or notorious) person, keep up with daily news on outlets to your point of view, explore the whole world. See chapter 20 on telecommunications.

Space. It may seem that you don't have enough space, especially if you had to downsize. In actuality you have more space than you use. If you have two or more bedrooms, you only use one. The others are set aside as guest bedrooms for visiting family or a storeroom, a sewing room, or a pool room. Every night you sleep on the same side of the same bed in the same room with the same still life on the wall. In the morning, you pull clean clothes from the same side of the closet. Extra closets have extra clothes. The living room has a sofa and three chairs, but you sit in the same place every evening.

In your individual space, you must combat the ravages of loneliness. You must find worthwhile human contacts throughout the week, and you have to find ways to turn your alone time into meaningful solitude.

Have a focal point of beauty, something that reminds you that you are home, a good place to be. A picture on the wall is the most obvious. You may already have one. If not, look in online catalogs of art work or art books borrowed from the library. Pick several possibilities. As you come back to them time after time, see which one most sustains your interest. You want something you can look at repeatedly, something which will offer a new perspective in light or coloring or substance with new viewings. You may choose a family photograph, recent or old. I have a picture of my father when he was thirty, not yet married, on a construction site with a lunch bucket in his hand. Some possibilities for that focal point include:

o a single carnation from the grocery, inexpensive and lasting three weeks
o a statuette of St. Francis, inspiring peace, forgiveness, nature
o a lava lamp, much scorned by contemporary designers, for the seeker of a show of light and form
o a crewel embroidery or cross-stitch, created either by yourself or someone dear
o a Play-doh car, formed by a grandchild
o a geranium on the windowsill, provided you can keep such things alive
o a fish tank with tropical species, with the same caution
o a set of drapes or curtains on the window, bought because they pleased your eye

We could go on forever. The world is full of beautiful things, all in the eye of the beholder. Let something speak to you, and it will continue to speak when you have procured it and placed it in your home. If one focal point loses its charm, give it away and be on the lookout for another.

Structure. Plan a loose structure for your time. See the sample below.

o A. Start with your meals, whether three or more. Plan a specific time of day for those meals.
o B. Put in appointments and other can't-miss times, for example, the dentist on Tuesday.
o C. Put in goals at a certain time each day— straightening, meditation or exercise, reading, making contacts. Note that because of the dentist on Tuesday, some things had to be rearranged and others dropped.

- o D. If there are other things you want to do, you can add them to the schedule.
- o Either fill in the remaining blanks with things you want to do, such as shopping, or go from our basic structure on an hour-by-hour basis.

	M	Tu	W
9:00 AM	A breakfast	A breakfast	A breakfast
10:00 AM	C straighten		C straighten
11:00 AM		B dentist	
12:00 PM	C meditate/ exercise		C meditate/ exercise
1:00 PM	A lunch	A lunch	A lunch
2:00 PM	D read	C meditate/ exercise	D read
3:00 PM	C email/phone	C email/phone	C email/phone

The advantage of living alone is that you can set the structure, decide when to deviate from it, make adjustments in your lifestyle. If you spend the day in your pajamas, nobody will complain. If you spend every day in your pajamas, you have to decide if you want this to be your lifestyle, or if you want to adopt a new pattern. It is up to you.

Look at the structure for the day each morning and see that it is satisfactory. A special activity, such as going shopping with your daughter, may throw everything else off. Accommodate for that.

Lonely time. Identify the time of day when you feel particularly lonely, when the blues overtake you, and plan especially for that time. It may be the morning when the day stretches ahead, or the evening when everything is quiet. Mine is late afternoon, when the day is not quite done but my energy has been spent, waiting for the end of day when I can drop the "shoulds."

Rain can intensify loneliness, especially a cold rain. Going out is not inviting. The air inside is damp, chill. You can hear the water running down the gutter, the slick sound car tires make.

Once you have identified your vulnerable time of day, you can develop a plan of attack to help you get through it. Plan to be busy, to be absorbed in something, but in a pleasant way. If instead you reach a point during the day when you slump down on the couch with a big sigh and say, "Now what?" then you will find it much more difficult to re-attach yourself to the day.

Be prepared. Have a space already cleared on the table. If your plan is to make beaded jewelry, have the beads in a case that you can lift to the table. If your plan is to e-mail friends, create a short list of things you can write about.

Suppose one day I plan to catch up on the mail that has been accumulating for two weeks. I first clear a space on the coffee table, mostly by moving other things around. I find the mail and put it in a loose stack. I go over in my mind the steps I want to take.

1. I place the accumulated mail on the lower right corner of the table.
2. * I open the first envelope.
   a. If it can be discarded, I do so. It is a week before the elections and the beginning of Medicare open enrollment, so there is a lot to toss out.
   b. If it is a bill, I put it mid-table above the stack of mail.
   c. If it is something to take care of later (to read, answer, think about), I put it to the left of the stack of mail.
   d. If it is something that can be filed without further action, I put it to the far left of the table.
3. I repeat from * until the stack of mail on the right is gone.
4. Then I pay the bills. If paying by mail, I go so far as to put stamps on the envelopes and set them by the door. I put the kept portion of the bills in the "to be filed" stack.
5. I sift through the stack in the middle set aside for later. I find the easiest things to do and take care of them. I work my way through the stack, setting aside to file when necessary. I go until the stack is empty. Anything left over becomes clutter.
6. I file the last stack.

Your lonely time can be used for whatever helps you. More tips on how to handle (and embrace) solitude can be found in a previous chapter. You may also want to use this time to rest or sleep.

Maintain social contacts. 48% of men living alone and 71% of women living alone report that they are satisfied with the number of friends they have. [American Psychological Association, op. cit.] If you are without social contacts, you may opt to take corrective actions as described later in this book.

Golden years. Your personal living situation can be the single greatest factor in determining your enjoyment in these years. Consider the following:

- How much can you take care of?
- If you will need help, where will it come from?
- How much emotional support can you count on from friends, family, neighbors, caregivers?
- What options are financially feasible?
- Will you need to change your living arrangement at some point? In how long?

Once you have planned to spend these golden years in the best place suited to you, they can in fact be a blessing.

Challenge for Change. Especially if you live alone, sit somewhere different this evening, even if only for an hour. See the room from a new perspective.

12. Institutional Living

There were a hundred and forty-two staircases at Hogwarts: wide, sweeping ones; narrow, rickety ones; some that led somewhere different on a Friday; some with a vanishing step halfway up that you had to remember to jump. Then there were doors that wouldn't open unless you asked politely, or tickled them in exactly the right place, and doors that weren't really doors at all, but solid walls just pretending.
J. K. Rowling, *Harry Potter and the Sorcerer's Stone.*

Institution. An institution is considered to be a special place for the care or support of persons who are no longer able to or no longer want to live independently. They are buildings of various sizes with multiple rooms (like a hotel) for residents to live singly or doubly. Typically they serve meals either in a dining room or bedside. Their staff administers a certain level of care, depending on the nature of the institution.

Assisted living is probably the least lonely environment. It consists of a large structure similar to an apartment building. They offer two-bedroom units, one-bedroom units, and (more commonly) studios. The studio is one large room with bed, dresser, and comfy chair for daytime. They vary in size even within one facility and may have room for a dinette or a desk. Usually a corner kitchenette with a microwave and half-size refrigerator/freezer is included. It can have a private bathroom or a "jack and jill" bathroom which is shared with the unit next door on one side.

The difference between independent and dependent living depends on the type and amount of assistance you receive. Assisted living typically provides housecleaning, a change of linens, and laundry. At intake you are assessed to determine which Activities of Daily Living (ADLs, as listed in the previous chapter) you need help with, for example, dressing or bathing. Facilities vary on incontinence care. They also vary on what is included in the basic monthly price and which ADLs and other services have an add-on fee. Transportation to shopping and other outside events can also be provided at no extra cost or with a fee. In comparing the costs of two similar facilities, you need to go beyond the monthly fee and find out what it includes.

Other on-site amenities may include a barber/beauty shop or devotional services. A podiatrist, dentist, or other professionals may have office hours on-site. A few facilities have a whirlpool or pool. The staff usually tries to keep the place lively with extra events and seasonal decorations. You need to shop for a facility starting with a checklist of what amenities are important to you.

In order to compare costs, find out what the monthly fee will be, what it includes, how much for additional services. Get all costs added and quoted as monthly. Genworth Cost of Care Survey reports that the nationwide average in 2019 was $4051/month for a studio for assisted living. The least expensive was an average of $2880/month in Minnesota, the most expensive $11,287/month in the District of Columbia. If you have family members in more than one state, whom you choose to live with might mean a difference of cost. Costs can vary between the same localities also.

Places to meet people:

Dining room. Eat meals with the community. If the food is bad, take at least one meal a day in the dining room. On their websites some facilities boast of having a chef to prepare their meals. During the initial tour of the facility, often free lunch is provided so that you can sample the cooking.

Common areas. Some facilities have only one common area with the television blaring for the hard of hearing. Chairs all face the same way, not conducive to chatting.

Often you find another open area in addition to the TV room, or perhaps the dining room is open to residents outside of meal hours. Go here to socialize, to sit near people, maybe to strike up a conversation. As people see you more often, as your face becomes more familiar, they trust you more and are more willing to open up to you. Be patient, but be persistent.

Activities. The range of daily activities offered also varies greatly from facility to facility. Some offer games like bingo, crafts, physical and occupational therapy, exercise or yoga groups, discussion groups. You can meet people and appease your loneliness. Even if you have to push yourself at first, it is better to go to a few groups than to stay in your room.

I know one person who left the door open to her room. One or two people would stop by to chat. Several others greeted her as they passed. She watched the activities of the corridor, the passage of meal carts and staff and residents. She did not feel lonely.

Visit one-on-one like the neighbors that you are. When they return the visit, offer beverages, if only tap water with a cube of ice.

In order to avoid loneliness, you need to go to where the people are. It is tempting to procrastinate because it is difficult to expose yourself to other people that way. What if they reject you?

The odds of that happening are not high. People are, well, human, with their own fears of rejection. They want to be accepted by you. Remember that smile. Make the effort. Otherwise you can spend days, even weeks, in misery, alone in your room waiting to assimilate. Gaining friends is the hardest thing you've had to do since your family moved in third grade and you had to walk into a classroom of strangers, but that worked out

Skilled nursing facility. Let me tell you about my friend Joan's experience. Joan was ambulatory when she entered the nursing home, but she gained more weight and had opportunity to exercise less, with the result that she eventually needed a wheelchair to get around. She couldn't propel it herself and was dependent on having someone push her where she wanted to go.

One day when I visited we were discussing the Catholic mass and the feasibility of going together. I couldn't get her wheelchair into my car; therefore the possibility of taking her with me was out. On the other hand, the nursing home had a Catholic communion service every Sunday. Volunteer lay people from the local parish brought host that had already been consecrated, sang songs, read readings, and distributed the Eucharist. Joan and I exchanged the kiss of peace.

On Sunday mornings I came to Joan's room to take her to the communion service. Usually she was dressed and in her wheelchair. Sometimes the staff had forgotten, and Joan had no way to measure the days and never knew when Sunday came.

Joan would have benefited from physical therapy to help her maintain her mobility or at least a walking regimen. They did not appear to engage her in a way to maintain her cognitive skills or to associate with others. In her last years she underwent a period of adequately-cared-for decline.

She had a brother one hundred miles away who received reports from staff. Those of us who visited a few hours a week did not impact her overall lifestyle or her care.

In February one year I moved two thousand miles away. I wrote Joan a letter that May, figuring that someone would read it to her, but it was returned unopened. When I checked with the nursing home, I learned that in April she had "died in her sleep."

Joan's experience appears to be typical of that of a skilled nursing facility. The staff had an underlying layer of genuine kindness (not always the case) in spite of being harried and efficient. Needs of the moment were attended to. I didn't see evidence of a plan for long-term needs. Nobody was helping her stay mobile.

In the semi-private room she had experienced a variety of roommates, some with too-loud television who sat glued to the screen and did not converse, some literally comatose. I was unaware of any roommate with whom she had bonded. Because of space constraints, it is not always possible for family to advocate for a change of roommate.

Loneliness was not recognized for the physical health hazard that it presents. Blood pressure is taken often and treated if necessary. The necessity for being with other people should be treated as well. The staff was efficient and kind but not pro-active.

Could I have done more? I would have had to get from Joan some legal status that enabled me to discuss her situation and activities with the staff and make suggestions. Perhaps a simple consent for Release of Information would have been sufficient, or maybe a power of attorney initiated by Joan with her brother's consent. The goal would be for staff to get Joan out into the community more. If I ever came across a similar situation, I will try to get more involved if the resident agrees.

If the family wants to keep the resident viable, plan frequent family visits as well as family involvement in treatment planning such as how often the resident is taken to a common area. At the least, meals should be taken in the dining room. Look for grounds or a neighborhood to walk. Seek a facility in which both the patient and the family (if available) meet with the staff for a regular update. Some states require this.

According to Genworth's Cost of Care Survey, the average national cost in 2019 for a semi-private room in a skilled nursing facility was $7513/month. Often this is paid for by Medicaid if the person has no assets.

Places to meet people. If you are capable of leaving your room, see the suggestions for assisted living. If you can't leave your room, chat with everyone who comes in—the person who makes up the bed, people who take vital signs or bring your meal. Use the telephone to invite outside people over. Tell them how much it would mean.

Rights. Institutional living facilities are licensed by the state in which the facility is situated. Each state has client rights for institutions such as board and care homes, assisted living facilities, and skilled nursing facilities. You should be given a copy of your resident rights when you first enter the facility. These may have variations from the client rights specified by the state. Check with the state ombudsperson to find out rights granted by the state.

Essentially you have the right to the decision-making capabilities of being a person so long as you are legally a person. That status changes if a court appoints a guardian. Also, if you have an advance directive, it may be in effect if you are unable to make decisions.

Some states' rights include the right:
o to be treated with respect
o to participate in treatment planning
o to refuse specific treatments (including electrocon-vulsive therapy)
o to refuse medications
o to see records

Does a person have a right to request to be trans-ferred from bed to wheelchair, to be taken somewhere? In Joan's case it took two men using a hoist to transfer her. They did it on Sundays when I was there. I suspect that much of the rest of the time neither the staff nor Joan wanted to be bothered. Some encouragement would have helped.

If it doesn't feel right, if it feels like you are being forced into a corner that doesn't fit, you can ask first to speak to the facility's resident advocate. If still not satis-fied, you can ask to speak to the state ombudsperson. The facility should help you do that, even placing the call for you if you desire.

Rights are an important part of your growth pro-cess when you reside in a facility.

Elder abuse can be found in any of the levels of living listed above, from independent living all the way down to skilled nursing facility. It can occur at the hands of family members as well as institutional caregivers. The types of elder abuse follow.
o *physical*: hitting, slapping, pushing, burns, gripping, etc.

o *emotional (psychological)*: yelling at, calling names, threatening, intimidating, ignoring, keeping wanted visitors away, etc.
o *sexual*: forcing to watch or participate in sexual acts including unwanted touching of sexual parts
o *neglectful*: doesn't try to respond to need
o *financial*: money or belongings are stolen or misappropriated

One sign of elder abuse is a feeling of fear or distress. At that point you need to consider getting help. See the numbers below.

Telephone numbers.
National Center on Elder Abuse: 855-500-3537
National Adult Protective Services Organization: 217-523-4431
National Long-Term Care Ombudsman Resource Center: 202-332-2275

Challenge for Change. If you live in an institutional setting, give it a homey touch—a plant, a picture on the wall or dresser, something created by your grandchild. Talk about it to people who come to your room.

Chapter 13. Dining Alone

> *For I have known them all already, known them*
all:--
> *Have known the evenings, mornings, afternoons,*
> *I have measured out my life with coffee spoons:*
> T. S. Eliot, "The Love Song of J. Alfred Prufrock"

Food and people go together. Whether the potluck is the excuse and the people are the means, or the business meeting is the reason and the box of doughnuts on the conference table is incidental; whether the food draws the people, or the gathering of people opts for food, people and food go together. The focus of family life is the dinner table.

On the other hand, you are one person, but you need to eat. You have a body which requires consistent replenishment, like the coal furnace that drives the steam engine that pulls the train. The next car behind the engine is the coal car, a ton of coal constantly fed into the furnace to provide the heat to make the steam.

You require nourishment on a daily basis. One survey reported that Americans are now eating only two meals a day with snacks filling the interim. A nutritional report suggests that the ideal is five small meals in a day. In this country we tend to think of the traditional as three meals a day: breakfast, lunch, dinner.

Whatever the distribution, the general principle is the same. Calories taken in need to be roughly the same as calories burned in the activities of the body. Dietary regimes differ according to metabolism and exercise. By now you know your body and know what works best for you in terms of weight maintenance.

Magazines sold at supermarkets and countless articles online give the basics of nutrition: If you eat meat, then lean meats are better. Eat lots of fruits and veggies. Avoid fatty foods and too many carbs. Fish oils are good. Drink lots of water.

Where to eat. One option is to eat in the living room while watching television. It may get messy, and you can't get that feeling of taking a break if you spend your mealtime in the same place as you spent your morning or afternoon. Being in a rut is an invitation to a feeling of loneliness.

You could opt to eat at the dinette set that has two chairs tucked in a corner between the kitchenette and the living room. You might have to share it with a stack of unopened mail. Push the mail to one side, and set a placemat on the other side to claim it as your own. You can browse through the mail as you eat, pulling out the obvious losers.

Or you can use the time to catch up on your favorite newspaper or magazine, something you will throw away in case it gets splattered with spaghetti sauce. Choose a magazine like *People* that will lie flat, not something like a fashion magazine that you will have to hold open with one hand.

Or choose the moment just to be. Appreciate the green beans as you pick them up with a fork. Enjoy the crunch of the chicken as you bite into the drumstick. Chase down the strands of spaghetti as you twirl them on a spoon. Meditate on the day.

You could make it an experience of mindfulness. Put on soft music, light a candle, and surround yourself with the physical sensations of your meal. It's as if your environment itself was your dining companion, familiar but new each evening,

Wherever you eat, remind yourself that this is okay with me. I am enjoying my meal; I am fine.

What to eat. Breakfast is the easiest meal. Too early in the morning for decision-making, most people tend to slip into a routine. For all the time I knew her, my mother had tea with lemon and sugar and a slice of buttered toast for breakfast. Even if she fixed a stack of pancakes for the rest of the family, when the meal was over and cleaned up, she had her tea and toast. Traditional choices include cereal (hot or cold), eggs, bagels. You can have nontraditional breakfasts, with leftover pizza being at the top of the list.

Lunch. Keep lunch simple—soup, sandwich, something you find in the fridge.

Recipe: take two slices of bread. Place two slices of cheese between them. Wrap in a paper towel and microwave on high for 14 seconds.

Dinner. If you are out running errands, you may want to pick up fast food for a change of pace. It is not recommended as a steady diet, and it can get expensive.

At home you can get delivery of pizza and Chinese food almost anywhere. Other apps for takeout food delivery: Grubhub and Seamless, UberEats, DoorDash, BeyondMenu, Postmates [source: *The Week*]. Check on delivery fees and reckon on the tip.

You may be eligible for the Meals on Wheels program. The nature of the program varies in different localities and even within a city. Some are subsidized nonprofits, and participants must be below a certain income level. Others are for-profit and charge for the meals. Often you can find a sample menu for the month online.

Many groceries have a full aisle of frozen entrees boxed in single servings. Many people eat alone, whether living alone or part of a multi-tasking family. The variety is endless. Some meals, such as chicken pot pie, include protein and veggies. All boxes have information on calories and fat content.

Boxes of frozen vegetables are in another aisle. By itself a box of corn or green beans or Brussels sprouts is sufficient for a meal.

Real food. Cooking for one is possible. I did it when my then-husband was in the navy and out to sea much of the time. The trick is to fix four portions of anything–casseroles, pork chops, meatloaf, fish. Eat two portions on two successive nights and freeze two for heating in the microwave later.

A whole chicken divides nicely into four quadrants, two breast and two back with the legs attached.

Make more of spaghetti sauce with or without ground beef. Freeze the extra in small square plastic containers. Whenever you want it, you will have the right amount to heat in the microwave and pour over a plate of spaghetti.

Recipe: In the microwave, melt a tablespoon of margarine in the bottom of a bowl. Drain one-half block of soft tofu and place in bowl. Crumble with a fork. If desired sprinkle with garlic salt or favorite herb or spice. Experiment each time you prepare it. You still have the other half of the block of tofu for another night. If desired (and not vegan) top with cheese. Microwave for 1 minute on high.

This meal in itself is filling. You will want to add fruits and veggies at some other time. Eat an apple in the afternoon. Or have a can of peaches in light syrup for dessert. Or a squeeze-tube of applesauce. Or have a salad for lunch. Or have a carrot any time. Or a banana.

Buying groceries. If you are mobile, have a car, and can keep track of things, you have the luxury of walking up and down the aisles of the store and seeing what's new. It may seem more hassle than luxury, but when your ability to go out is gone, you will miss it. Even when my memory was good, I needed a list. You may want a personal foldable cart in the back of the car to carry the groceries up.

We've already discussed frozen boxes of vegetables. Also in the canned goods aisle you can generally find a shelf of smaller cans of vegetables--peas, spinach, mixed vegetables. Creamed peas are better from canned peas than from frozen peas.

Perhaps you need help with your groceries, either someone to take you to the store or someone to go to the store for you. Family members often step up to the plate on this one. In my senior building on Sunday afternoon I often see two generations bringing in a personal cart of groceries. The son often has the toilet paper tucked under his arm because there is no room in the cart.

Alternatively you can hire a caregiver to do your grocery shopping for you. They are happy to take your list and go. You will have to decide whether to have cash on hand for the groceries or to trust her with your debit card. Check the receipt. Hire someone from a bonded agency.

More and more supermarkets deliver groceries and Amazon Fresh does as well. Some questions you need to ask:

- o Is there an overhead? InstaCart is annual; Amazon is monthly.
- o Is there a delivery fee? Does it include tip?
- o Is there a minimum order? Sometimes the minimum is too high for a single person.
- o How long in advance do I need to order?

o How do I order? Sometimes an app is needed.

. The answers aren't easy to find. Some places
want you to do a trial period at promotional rates and
then tell you the ongoing rate later. Be careful of the trial
period which may automatically bill you an enrollment
fee after the trial period has ended.

I order from InstaCart every two weeks and find it
a reasonable way to get my groceries. Packed together,
the frozen food stays frozen upon delivery. The ice cream
is harder than if I'd brought it from the store. Even eggs
are usually unbroken. Bananas are a little beaten up but
still good. Most of the produce is in reasonable condition.
I may look around at other options at some point.

Dining out alone. You haven't experienced eating
alone to the fullest until you have dined out by yourself.
In making plans to dine alone, one fears looking conspic-
uous if not weird, but that needn't be. The person who
looks askance at you is not judging you because you are
alone; rather that person is taking you in because you are
part of their surroundings as they are part of yours. You
are not dining alone. You are dining with an entire roomful of people. You just don't know their names.

After a couple of false starts trying to arrange
transportation, I decided on a self-proclaimed bistro within walking distance of my place in an area of small shops
and eateries. The bistro turned out to be closed on Sunday—poor research on my part. With a computer you can
find hours open, menu, and prices. Often there are photos
showing the restaurant and what people generally wear.

Nail down your destination in advance. If you are
undecided on where to go when you set out, you will
wander or drive around and settle on carry-out at home.

Map your route. I wound up a couple of blocks down at Giuseppe's Pizzeria.

Dining in a sit-down restaurant (as opposed to picking up at the counter) follows a typical pattern in America almost regardless of ethnicity. When you arrive you are usually greeted by someone who seats you or takes your name. The person looks around you and behind you and asks, "How many?"

"Just one," you say with confidence. So long as you intend to pay your bill, you have every right to enjoy the experience of dining in this restaurant. The trend is catching on. Between 2014 and 2016 the number of one-person reservations rose 62%.

When seated you are given a menu, and the waitperson arrives to ask if you would like a beverage (alcoholic or non). If you like, you can initiate small talk which will continue throughout the meal. As she gets your beverage, you look over the menu. You decide if you want an appetizer. You look over the entrees, the sandwiches, the salads, quickly deciding against more than half.

You could have avoided this step by checking the menu online at home. When the waitperson brings your beverage, she asks if you are ready to order. It is okay to ask for a little more time. You may want to ask your waitperson about one or more of the dishes.

I narrow it down to two or three and pick one arbitrarily. I can always come back some other time for another choice.

Once you have ordered, your time is free until your food is brought, usually ten minutes or more. Take in the décor or theme, the walls, the furnishings, any scattered ornamentation, the lighting, the tableware. Is there music?

Giuseppe's had soft rock. Hanging diagonally in three corners were large-screen televisions showing basketball, soccer, and NASCAR. In the back were beer and wine on one side and a counter with the cash register on the other. Behind each of these was a wall-size blackboard written on with thick white chalk. Beer and wine specials were posted on the left and dinner specials on the right. Happy hour is M-F 4:30-5:30 p.m.

Tables and chairs were arranged to the side of the room. In the center stood stools and three long tables resting on massive beer kegs. Nobody sat at these.

You can also use the time to people-watch. I gazed around the lightly populated room freely. Everybody was absorbed in their own table. Nobody met my eye. If they had I would have nodded in recognition and looked away.

Almost all were in their twenties or thirties. To my left was a pair of women sharing a pizza. To my right was the only other person alone, a woman reading a book with a library binding. She had just ordered. Past her was a perfect family—mom, dad, grade school girl and boy.

On the middle of the opposite wall sat the only other elderly person, a woman in her eighties with a smart strawberry perm. All along the wall behind her as far as the window clustered ten or so young adults of both genders with uniformly dark hair. Grandma's birthday? They soon left and then stopped outside for a group photo which the waitperson snapped.

In the far corner sat a couple with a pizza. They seemed pretty used to each other, no handholding or soulful gazing. Stopping on the way home from Lowe's?

I had brought a magazine to read, but I started taking notes instead. Perhaps they thought I was a food critic.

Bring something, such as a magazine or your hat, that you can leave on the table. If you go to the restroom, it will show that that you are not finished.

The server brought a juicy pepperoni pizza to the reader on my right. She propped the book open on her lap and leaned its top against the table as she ate.

In due course my veggie sandwich was brought. It was on a full-size submarine bun sliced in half, so packed that when I took a bite tomatoes, lettuce, onions, green peppers, and avocado slithered out of the edges. Also on the plate was a salad of chopped lettuce and tomatoes with vinaigrette dressing.

Practice mindfulness as you slowly eat. Savor the tastes, the aromas, the textures, the temperatures. Continue to look around.

The family on the right had left and been replaced by another perfect family across the room where grandma had been. The couple in the corner dialogued between bites of pizza. The women on my left boxed up half the pizza with the help of the waitperson and left. A small man with dark hair and mustache came out from the kitchen area and cleared their plates and glasses. I conjectured that he also cooked. Perhaps he was Giuseppe himself.

The waitperson brought a container for the other half of the sandwich. At this point you can decide whether to prolong your experience with dessert or coffee. I chose neither. The check was brought in a vinyl folder the size of a passport.

If you want to pay with cash, slip some bills inside the folder. The waitperson will collect the folder and bring it back with your change. Put the tip inside the folder and leave it on the table.

If you prefer to pay with plastic, put your credit/debit card inside the folder. The waitperson will bring it back with a receipt showing the total for the meal and a space for tip and final total. Write in the tip and total, sign one copy of the receipt and leave it in the folder on the table. Keep the duplicate.

The usual tip it is 15-20%. Even if the service was barely adequate, rarely do you go below that. You may want to go higher.

As I left, I reflected it had certainly been better than spending a gloomy afternoon at home with a cheese sandwich. The book reader had finished her pizza and had about twenty pages to go in her book. I hadn't felt awkward in my aloneness. I think the reason was that I was directed outward, paying close attention to my surroundings rather than worrying about my feelings of inadequacy.

Would I do it again? I have to admit that it was fun, but the total tab came to about $15.00. For that I can get three frozen meals and a two-liter of diet Coke. I have to convince myself that it's okay to splurge once in awhile, perhaps mark it in my calendar once a month. I highly recommend the experience.

Challenge for Change. Have something different for dinner, something you never had before, whether at home or out.

Chapter 14. Sleeping Alone

Slow -- Night -- that must be watched away --
As Grains upon a shore --
Too imperceptible to note --
Till it be night -- no more –
Emily Dickinson, "A Night -- there lay the Days between"

Monasticism. Maybe you have been without a bed partner for a long time—perhaps always—or maybe you are only now getting used to it. Either way you have plenty of mattress space to toss and turn, and you find yourself flailing about seeking a position where your body can be at rest. You have felt mostly tired the next day, and all you are asking for is a decent night's sleep so that you can function in the morning.

Sufficient sleep. How do you know you've had enough sleep? Basically when you are refreshed the next day, have energy to get done most of what you want to get done, can face the day with a sense of challenge. Estimates of the amount necessary vary, but generally 7-8 hours is considered a healthy minimum. If your sleep has been interrupted, it is hard to be sure how much you've slept.

The question is whether you go through the day feeling like a dish of melting ice cream, operating from an outside dimension, using remote-controlled robot hands to scrape the carrots, pausing in your tracks until you remember what you were doing. Making a phone call to the pharmacy seems like too much effort, and you procrastinate if not fail in the task. Like an electric car, you need time to recharge the batteries or you can't function properly.

According to the National Sleep Foundation [2009], in addition to daytime drowsiness, symptoms of lack of sleep can include loss of memory, concentration problems, irritability, depression, and confusion. Loss of sleep is considered to be a contributing factor to dementia.

Night time. The world around you spends one-third of its time in the oblivion of sleep. This sleep serves as the world's down time when stores and offices are closed, families are silent, and personal contacts unavailable. Even if you know someone who is often awake at 3:00 am, you don't want to contribute to their sleep disruption. If you are not participating in sleep during some or all of the world's down time, it becomes for you an alone time.

Medical problems. Many medical problems interfere with regular sleep: sleep-disordered breathing (includes apnea), repetitive leg movements (includes restless leg syndrome), motor activity while dreaming, dementia. Also medical illness such as pain (includes arthritis, back pain), shortness of breath, the night need to go to the bathroom, neurological deficits (includes Parkinson's), and depression can be a factor.

If insomnia is chronic (three times per week for three months or more according to the *Diagnostic and Statistical Manual*), you should consult a doctor. Don't accept a scrip for meds and a pat on the back. Your specific disorder needs to be diagnosed and treated. Treatments should address the primary problem and not the complaint itself.

Circadian rhythm. Your circadian rhythm which regulates your day/night cycle is located in a part of the brain called the hypothalamus. It receives direct input from the eyes. A lower light condition signals the brain that it is time to get drowsy. If sleep is disturbed, try to maintain normal light/dark sequences. Take a walk in late afternoon or early evening. The sunlight as well as the exercise will be beneficial.

A common example of circadian rhythm is jet lag. The clock on the airport wall says 9:00 pm, but your body says 6:00 pm. You experience hunger rather than tiredness.

One disturbance of circadian rhythm is when you feel the need to go to bed earlier than is common each evening, perhaps at seven or eight in the evening. The result is that you awake fully recharged at three or four in the morning. You have about three hours to face while the world is still down.

You can try to go to bed later each night in increments until you get back on a more regular sleep schedule. Or you can learn to use the alone time in ways that satisfy you. Tape the baseball game and watch it during your awake hours.

Often sleep is interrupted by sleep apnea or the need to go to the bathroom. When you can fall back asleep without difficulty, this is not serious. The problem arises when you have problems falling back asleep.

A similar problem is falling asleep to begin with. You go to bed at a normal time but find yourself still pounding the pillow two hours later. Both cases require some practice in falling asleep.

Falling asleep. Caffeine of course should be avoided several hours before attempting to sleep. No evening latte. Not all teas with fancy names (Darjeeling, Constant Comment for example) are herbal. Chocolate contains caffeine. That Hershey kiss on the pillow will have to wait until morning. Even a healthy-sounding soft drink like Sunkist has caffeine listed on the label. Know what you are imbibing.

Avoid alcohol and sleeping pills as sleep aids. They can induce the wrong kind of sleep which does not in fact recharge the batteries, and their effectiveness may be time-limited.

Looking at a bright light (including television or your telephone) within an hour of bedtime can inhibit the sleep signal. I have friends who fall asleep while watching television. It probably keeps their minds off their worries at the time, but they may be delaying the time that they fall asleep, and they are still receiving the stimulus of dialogue (and sirens and gunshots) as they sleep.

In the evening, make a list of the type of concerns that keep you awake at night: financial, medical, family, and so on. Make a commitment to address them the following day. If the thought comes to mind as you try to fall asleep, remind yourself that it's on the list. Roll over and close your eyes in a darkened bedroom. If you think of something that isn't on the list, promise yourself that you will address it the next morning. And go to sleep.

Some say do not nap at all so that you will be most tired at bedtime. Some say take an hour nap in midafternoon so that you are not geared to fighting fatigue when you go to bed. Experiment with what works for you. If day-sleeping means more awake time at night, settle for a thirty-minute "power nap" where you set an alarm to wake you after half an hour.

One thing that all the experts agree on is to use your bed only for sleeping and for sex. Don't read in bed, don't watch television, don't go to bed during the day.

Your body needs to associate your bed with the place to sleep.

Personal experience. I will be the first to admit I have poor sleep habits. I take a trazodone at 6 pm. By 9 or 10 the lines of the words are swimming across the pages of the book I am trying to read. When I put it down, I am asleep almost instantly, whether in bed or sometimes while still in the chair.

I awaken anytime between midnight and 2 am, and I get up. I regard this as a special time when I have no obligations, no constraints. I drink a cup of coffee. I read scripture. I may work a bit on a project or do the crossword puzzles I never allow myself during the day.

Or I may just think. As a writer, I am allowed to spend time sitting and thinking—of the world, of people, of stories I mean to write but seldom do. I realize that I should reform, give up the coffee, try to go right back to sleep when I awaken. I have not yet been able to give up my time of freedom. The to-do list does not dominate my life at night.

Usually I do manage to go back to bed for a shorter interlude, and I average six hours of sleep at night, sufficient to get me through the day. When I get less than five, I fall asleep, as my daughter says, at the drop of a hat, certainly while trying to read or write, or even at a group discussion or eating supper.

I have often said that lack of sleep is a poor man's alcohol. It creates a distance, takes the edge of feelings off the day. One moves through with a particular numbness. And it is addictive.

Going to sleep exercise. Lie in your usual sleeping position. Take a couple of deep breaths. Now flex your toes for three seconds. Hold them tightly curled. After three seconds, release them completely. Let them go.

Enjoy the sensation of release from tension for about ten seconds.

Do the same thing with your feet. Arch them tightly for three seconds. Relax for ten. Feel the lack of tension, the looseness of your feet.

Moving up your body, again repeat with ankles, then with forelegs. Your shins are so heavy that they melt into the mattress.

Fingers, hands, forearms, upper arms. All of them loose now, just hanging from you.

Move on to your torso. Abdomen--tighten and relax. Butt. Chest.

The back is difficult to tense because it is already tense. Arch it out like a cat. Then starting with the bottom vertebra, release each vertebra one by one until all are curved in.

Nearly done. You may have fallen asleep already. Shoulders. Neck. Face—eyes and mouth.

And relax. Feel the heaviness of your body. If any muscles have tensed up, go back and relax them again. Drift. Float. Let yourself sleep.

Continued wakefulness. If you do not fall asleep after twenty or thirty minutes, whether it is your first attempt or after interrupted sleep, get out of bed and do something boring. Do not look at the clock. Do not get anxious about time.

Let your thoughts wander, Think of good things that happened to you the day before, or the month, or the year, or even during your lifetime. Think of the good things to come—the forsythia, your granddaughter's wedding. Speculate on what you will eat in the next week. Remember that problems are safely held on your list. This unproductive thought time is appropriate for what should be down time.

Pick a fat book from the coffee table, the one with all the pictures of the Vatican gardens. Leaf through it. Pause at the striking views. I remember one night finishing Doyle's *The Hound of the Baskervilles* after midnight. Fascinated by the terror, I had been unable to stop turning pages until the conclusion. When I finally went to bed in the dark and in the quiet, I felt alone and scared. The Vatican gardens would have been a safer book.

Do easy crossword puzzles, or play solitaire with real cards on a real table. Make this time out of bed pleasant.

Let the night air chill you. Don't wrap up in a sweater or a shawl. When you go back to bed, you can snuggle in your blankets and appreciate their warmth. Stay relaxed. Stay with good thoughts. Don't reach for them, but let them drift through.

Wake up at the same time every morning. Consider a change in biorhythms. You got up at six every morning to go to teach school. Is there any harm in getting up at eight or even nine? You will be unable to make those early morning dentist appointments, but he is there all day. You can still be in sync with the rest of the world.

It may be you had fewer than seven hours of sleep, maybe far fewer. That's okay. You made it through the night without anxiety, without the dread of loneliness. It's one night. You are learning to manage your time of wakefulness to decrease the impact on the night. You are learning good sleep hygiene, and in time it may pay off with better sleep.

Sexuality Some are not sleeping alone, whether because they have the blessing of a relationship that has extended forty or fifty years or more, or they have moved on to new relationships. The news is that sexuality is alive and possible in older people. Whether it is desirable is a matter of personal choice and value systems.

Intimacy may take different forms as you age. An open discussion with your partner about intimacy may be beneficial.

Also changes in the vagina and erectile dysfunction can interfere with the expression of sexuality. Other medical conditions may also be problematic. Consult with your doctor if there are medical issues.

Challenge for Change. Think of one good thing that happened to you today. Save it for tonight if you need it.

15. Being Sick and Alone

And once the storm is over, you won't remember how you made it through, how you managed to survive. You won't even be sure, whether the storm is really over. But one thing is certain. When you come out of the storm, you won't be the same person who walked in. That's what this storm's all about.
        Haruki Murakami, Japanese writer

Sickroom. Being sick alone is the pits. If you want someone to lay a cool damp washcloth on your fevered brow, you have to do it yourself. If you want to know your temperature, you have to find the thermometer yourself. If you want the covers straightened and tucked back in, again it's up to you.

Having an illness means finding moments of strength against the hours of weakness. Fortunately it doesn't last forever. Either you get better, or you get help.

Be prepared. When you are sick, you may not have anyone to run to the store for you. While you are feeling well, lay aside some basic sickroom supplies:

    thermometer (and spare)
    medications for pain/fever: ibuprofen, acetamino-
    phen, aspirin
    pain relief patch
    hot/cold water bottle
    antihistamine
    decongestant
    cough lozenges

antacid
anti-nausea
anti-diarrhea
laxative
lotion
antiseptic cream/wipes
bandages
water with electrolytes
tea
broth, bouillon
noodle soup, ramen
rice, applesauce, crackers
extra box of tissues
extra toilet paper
wastebasket
book

Some of these are combined in one medication, for instance the antihistamine and the decongestant. Read labels to find out what they do. If you can't read those tiny labels, ask your pharmacist to help you select appropriate medications. I have a magnifying glass at home so I can read the directions.

Fighting the illness. When you are sick, rest as much as you can. Let your body fight its battles. Stay warm. You may opt for staying in bed, or you may choose to sit up with a blanket. If you can, drink plenty of fluids. Follow all those sickroom rules you have always heard.

Take it easy. Being sick is your experience of the moment. Accept it. It will be over in a measurable amount of time.

Keep your environment clean. Pick up the tissues. Take dishes to the kitchen. Tighten the bedcovers. Make yourself a comfortable space. Then lay back.

Being alone induces fear. What if I get so sick that I can't summon help if I need it? Is there someone you could ask to check in on your daily—a friend, a neighbor, a family member? In their compassion they would probably respond to your isolation. You would do the same for others if you could. The worst of the illness will probably be over in a few days.

Personal experience. One morning I felt out of it, not sick, nothing hurt, not head nor stomach, not even dizzy, but strange. By 9:30 I had cancelled my 12:30 therapist appointment. No reason except I didn't feel like going. I am not a person who cancels appointments easily.

At noon I was sitting in my chair when I let myself slither to the floor. I no longer had the strength to sit upright in the chair.

I crawled on the floor not sure where I was going. An inner voice told me to "push the button." I wear a medical alert device that my kids had insisted on, and I pushed the button.

"Did you fall?" a woman's voice asked from the speaker.

"No," I replied.

"Then how can I help?"

I didn't know what to answer because I didn't know what was wrong. "I'm on the floor and I don't know why."

"I'll send help."

I crawled over to the door and unlocked it. That's the last I remember. I wasn't aware of the arrival of the paramedics or the ride to the hospital.

I woke up in the hospital already hooked up to an IV. A nurse was urging me to change to a hospital gown.

"No, I'm not staying."

"Just for now to be more comfortable." I put on the gown and stayed for four days. I had a blood infection. Rather than evince itself as a temperature spike, it caused confusion and weakness. I don't know what would have happened if I hadn't pushed the button.

One must be extra cautious when sick and alone. At a minimum, try to have someone who is checking on you at least daily by phone. It is okay to raise a false alarm every now and then if it will help you insure that you signal when the need is present.

Chronic illness. The best you can do is to follow your doctor's orders. If she recommends a walk every day, then walk unless it's freezing cold or blazing hot or pouring rain. Find a companion to walk with. Get a dog to walk.

Follow dietary restrictions. I have watched someone pour salsa on a three-egg omelet and say, "My doctor would kill me if he knew." Actually it's not the doctor that will kill you.

Pain. You may have the experience of unremitting pain. What can I say? I am sorry that you hurt, truly sorry. Try to keep your spirits up.

If he hasn't already, your doctor may refer you to a doctor who is a pain management specialist. She may prescribe medication, and she may prescribe a round of physical therapy to strengthen the muscles that are holding you together. I went twice a week for eight weeks with Vivienne, paid for by insurance, and she helped.

Once the physical therapy sessions have stopped, the exercises must be continued at home. Vivienne gave me diagrams showing what exercises to do: flat on my back, leg lifts, two, three,…, lumbar rotations, two, three,…. Twice a day I lie on my back to take my meds and put in my eye drops. I am in a position to do my exercises then.

Even with such a routine, the temptation is to skip. To counter that, I fill in a weekly log showing when I have done my exercises and ridden my exercise bike. At the end of the week I email it to my son Mickey.

He takes his role as coach seriously. He will ask, "What happened?" if I have been shirking. I tell him, "Next time," and I do it next time. When I am tempted to skip, I have the thought that Mickey will find out. Accountability helps me stick with the exercise program. And my back and hip hurt less.

When to call the doctor. I hesitate to give medical advice based on my seat-of-the-pants experience. If you have a chronic condition (digestive, respiratory, heart, etc.), chances are you have already discussed with your doctor what warning signs for that condition would warrant a phone call. Blood from anywhere is not good. The word "prolonged" indicates trouble.

Actually you can call the doctor anytime the office is open. His staff will be more than willing to talk to you and give advice. They may make an appointment. The doctor may write a referral to a home health agency to provide a visiting nurse to stop by on a daily basis until the worst is over.

The staff may consult the doctor and call in a prescription for you. Have the name and phone number of a pharmacy that delivers ready when you call. Every town has at least one. If it is not your regular pharmacy, call them when you hang up from the doctor's office. Give your address and insurance information so that they can fill the prescription.

If you have a Medicare supplement, some plans have an ask-a-nurse program, usually 24/7. Check the back of your insurance card for information.

You can call the hospital emergency room just to get information and advice. If they suggest that you come in, decide on your means of transit. You can get a ride from someone or contact Lyft or Uber or call a private taxi. Always have money for two cab fares set aside. Remember your insurance cards and your ID. An ambulance is the last choice because of the expense and the feelings of anxiety.

Recovery. Once you have been advised and are settled in for the duration, all that's left is to wait the illness out. When you start to feel better, use your time as you would in moments of solitude. Keep yourself lightly amused. Make contact with people by phone. Don't push too much at first.

Now you have made it through. You may have been afraid, but you are stronger for the experience. If you ever have a friend who is sick, reach out to her at least by telephone.

Your body is a wonderful if contrary machine. Approach the new day.

Tricia. My friend Tricia wrote:

> Starting from the moment of birth until present day, I've experienced a multitude of health problems. Each diagnosis would be challenging to most adults. This includes three life-threatening illnesses and five chronic conditions. I have dealt with each primarily alone.
>
> Being sick and alone helped me to become an empowered patient. I stand up for myself with each doctor, healthcare worker and pharmacist. I

manage twenty medications a day, including packing, ordering and with the assistance of an alarm taking.

I believe it's time to take my life experiences and share with others. I want to teach others how to become empowered patients. My hope is to teach this class at Senior Centers, Hospital Patient Support Programs and College Extension Courses.

When I read the chapter title sick and alone, I thought of my most recent challenge, cancer, surgery followed by both radiation and chemo therapy. The worst by far was the incontinence caused by the radiation therapy. I was completely unprepared and I faced it completely alone. When I turned to my doctor I found her response unrealistic. I was left frustrated, angry and still alone.

Someone reminded me "I'm proactive" and asked how I plan to resolve the issue. Thus I went to my Doctor and shared my feelings. She heard me and tried to be understanding. I have followed up with suggestions about a better way of handling the problem in the future.

To top 2019 ended as badly as it began... On November 14 I had a bad fall and spent six days in a hospital followed by approximately five weeks in a rehab/convalescent home. Within the first 48 hours I realized my above mention seminar was to become a book first...

For the first time in decades I had lost my voice and my power, but I've found both facing cancer, then I was placed in a nursing home. I felt my very survival depended on becoming my own advocate... I doubt anyone at the hospital was prepared for a patient with a strong will and confidence. I had to fight for my room, medication and medication management.

This was made possible by my inner strength, years of experience dealing with the medical community and my good friends. Living alone is one thing, but knowing you have friends beyond the walls, is a blessing.

Challenge for Change. You have a job ahead of you. Make sure that you have all of the following information written down somewhere where you can get to it easily.

Primary care physician: name, phone number, address.
Other specialist(s): name, phone number, address.
Someone who can help: Name, phone number.
Urgent care: Name, phone number, address.
Emergency room: Hospital, phone number.
Pharmacy: Name, phone number.
Alternate pharmacy (delivers): Name, phone number.
Ask-A-Nurse: phone number.
Cash or credit card for cab.
ID and insurance cards.

Also have a list of the medications you take, the dose, the frequency for the hospital.

Chapter 16. Community Efforts

I alone cannot change the world, but I can cast a
stone across the waters to create many ripples.
Saint Teresa of Calcutta

Good news. We have been noticed. Increasingly
articles about the elderly speak of the problems of loneliness and the health consequences they bring. In some
places solutions are being offered:

AARP connect2affect: "Isolation is a growing
health epidemic. More than 8 million adults age 50 and
older are affected by isolation."

engAGED: "...remaining socially engaged im-
proves quality of life and is associated with better
health."

CareMore (Anthem): "We're trying to reframe
loneliness as a treatable medical condition that can be
treated."

SeniorServ: "UCLA researcher, Steve Cole, recently reported in a published study that 'social isolation
is the best-established, most robust social or psychological risk factor for disease out there. Nothing can com-
pete.'"

Humana: "In January 2019 the federal Health Resources & Services Administration used the term 'loneliness epidemic' to describe the situation among older
people, saying 43% of seniors reported feeling lonely on
a regular basis."

Some activities to engage seniors have existed for
some time, while others are emerging in response to the

new attention being paid to the problem. Many are local initiatives that are cropping up in various communities.

Meals on Wheels operates in 5,000 communities under the umbrella of various community organizations. Volunteers bring preselected full course meals to recipients in their homes. The cost to the recipient varies. Some programs are subsidized.

Although the meal assures adequate nutrition for the senior, a stated goal is also to reduce senior isolation. Usually the person bringing the meal takes time to chat with the person receiving it and to make sure that everything is okay.

The initiative has been in existence since started by a small group of Philadelphia citizens in 1954. It serves nearly 2.4 million seniors annually. Check in your community to see if Meals on Wheels is operating there.

engAGED is administered by the National Association of Area Agencies on Aging (n4a). It proposes to engage seniors in their communities by connecting them with volunteering. It appears to be geared toward those who are able to get out. Any grass-roots organization that offers such an opportunity is invited to become involved with engAGED if they agree with the guidelines. Partner organizations include Peace Corps 50+, Red Cross, and the United Way. Contact www.engagingolderadults.org, or n4a can be reached at 202-872-0888.

Friendly Visitor programs operate in several communities. Typically a volunteer is matched with a senior with similar interests. The volunteer visits at least twice monthly, and the two agree on what activities to pursue, whether to chat or play games or knit or take a stroll around the neighborhood. Google "Friendly Visitor" and the name of your community to see if there is a nearby program.

CareMore is a recent initiative of Anthem Insurance in recognition of the fact that loneliness and isolation have a direct impact on the health costs of seniors. It has identified 1,100 clients in four states for its initial efforts. These are focused on building personal connections with at-risk patients through consistent and positive engagement.

Local resources. Look to what might already exist in your community. Google your town's name along with such key words as "elderly" or "seniors" or "aged." Ask your Area Agency on Aging and your local library.

Call your city offices to see if they know of any programs for the elderly. Find out if there is an ecumenical council of churches. Catholic churches typically send out eucharistic ministers to shut-ins. What are other churches doing?

I know of a synagogue in Cleveland that sponsors a monthly "Pet Visit Sunday." Individuals and even whole families bring a "docile" dog or cat to visit with the residents of a retirement community.

Advocacy. If you are able to get out, attend the meetings of the town council and civic organizations. Ask what they are doing for the elderly. You may discover resources of which you were not aware. How can they be made better known?

Using the quotes at the beginning of this chapter, you may make people aware of the need. They may be willing to undertake a solution. Even something that impacts only a handful of seniors is a start.

The United Kingdom has an effort called Contact the Elderly. One Sunday per month on a rotating basis one person hosts an afternoon tea party for 4-8 seniors. The same volunteers drive the same guests every month so that there is continuity. They have tea and snacks and chat a while. The concept is simple, and yet since the first event in 1965 over 100,000 lonely elderly people have been served.

You don't have to start with 100,000. Interest one civic group in hosting one tea party (or coffee) monthly, and progress will have been made.

What other organizations could make a monthly visit to a skilled nursing facility? Every town has a garden club. On a certain day, encourage members to bring flowers cut from their gardens in biodegradable cups. You only need to call the president of the garden club to plant the seed (so to speak) for the idea.

The bridge group could play cards once a month, not just bridge but gin rummy and go fish and cribbage as well.

Imagine if there were a gourmet cooking group.

Computer savvy. Because it concentrates on finding community resources, this chapter more than others relies on the use of a computer to be effective. Some companies make "simpler" computers for seniors and other non-tech persons, simpler in that they don't have all the features.

Before you sell yourself short, go to the library and try out one of the computers there for public use. A librarian may be able to help you get started. If nothing else learn to look things up. A whole new world will open up for you. Ever wonder how many books are in the Library of Congress? There are nearly 145 million items, of which more than 33 million are books. I had the answer in the time it took to type the question.

Community colleges offer courses for using a personal computer. They sometimes give seniors a break on tuition.

Refurbished computers can sometimes be obtained free or at reduced prices. Contact Microsoft's refurbishment program at www.msregrefurb.com or Computers with Causes at www.computerswithcauses.org. Check on the web for other refurbishment programs.

Momentum. We have reached the tipping point where the problem of lonely elderly people is now in the news. Interested persons have started to seek a solution one person at a time. You can be a resource for them, explaining first-hand the impact of feelings of being cut off from the rest of the world.

Challenge for Change. Call your city government and ask what is being done for the socialization of the elderly.

17. Conversation

When a friend calls to me from the road
And slows his horse to a walk,
I don't stand still and look around
On all the hills I haven't hoed,
And shout from where I am, "What is it?"
No, not as there is a time to talk,
I thrust my hoe in the mellow ground,
Blade-end up and five feet tall,
And plod. I go up to the stone wall
For a friendly visit.
      "A Time To Talk," Robert Frost, *Robert Frost's Poems*

Connecting. A milkweed pod opens and releases its silks to the breeze, where the white puffs dance and bob on the currents. Two or more come together, their waxy filaments touching, so that they form one cluster rising on the air. Conversation follows this pattern of disparate units connecting. You and another person or persons are sharing your beings for a time. Both are uplifted.

To be less lonely, you make more connections, conversations you engage in during the course of a day. Some will remain strangers; some become casual acquaintances; some, if you are open to it, will become friends. At the least, in the evening when you look back upon the day, you will recall that encounter with another person.

Generosity. Are you feeling generous today? Conversation means giving of yourself to the person(s) involved, even if they are not responding fully.

o Attention. Put aside extraneous thoughts as you do in meditation. Concentrate on the verbal and non-verbal signals--the words spoken, the tone of voice, the facial expression, the body language. Experience what the person is saying. Put aside distractions like cell phones.

o Empathy. You hear the words and relate to what they mean to the speaker. "My cat is sick," he says. You have no pet, but you understand that he fears a loss. You put yourself in his shoes.

o Feedback. You let him know that you heard and you understand. You may express empathy with his concerns. You may show interest by asking questions, for instance, the age of the cat. You leave the door open for him to speak further about the cat.

All of these you give to him from your inner self. You reach in and find your own feelings to give back to him so that he feels affirmed.

When you are the one to introduce a topic, you gauge his feelings on the topic and keep it to common ground.

You can afford to be generous. You have treasures enough within you that you can give without being depleted, treasures of listening and compassion and relating. At the start of a conversation, say to yourself, "I value this person and want to give to him." Then relax and let it happen. At the same time, feel free to have an unannounced time limit.

Purposes. Three purposes can be defined by conversation:

1. *To connect with another person.* Standing in close proximity, you can make some internal observations about another person: tall, slumped, flip-

flops, fancy watch. Based on these observations you may make assumptions, valid or otherwise: basketball player, tired, casual, rich. Not until you and that person exchange information do you truly find out more about him: mathematician, gently assertive, father. His watch belonged to his father. As you converse, you are also offering glimpses of yourself. You and the other person are connecting.

2. *To transfer information, feelings, views.* You may give your boss the information that the project will be completed on time. You may tell a friend that you are happy with your new apartment. You may tell a fellow party-goer your view that the music is too loud. You give to the other person from what is within you.

3. *To strengthen the bond.* When you converse with a stranger, for instance at the supermarket check-out, this doesn't usually happen. You are ships passing in the night, probably never to meet again. When you find yourself associating with a person frequently, say on the bus, you gradually reveal more about yourselves as you converse and move toward friendship.

Sakyong Mipham said, "It's not necessarily what we're talking about, it's how we talk about it that affects us. It's about the caring within the words. As we are drawn out of ourselves, we become more other-centered. And this is the key to conversation, to appreciate the one in front of you, which creates a moment of happiness for both."[9]

Hypothetical conversation. We will follow along as two imaginary persons have a conversation. Alice and

---

[9] Sakyong Mipham, *The Lost Art of Good Conversation*, p. 18

Brenda meet in a downtown office elevator lobby. They
have never met before. Alice decides to start small talk
while they are waiting. She picks a classic opener, the
weather.

Alice: *This is a lot of rain we are having.*

As in good conversation, Alice speaks slowly and
distinctly while making good eye contact. She speaks
loudly enough to be heard in the busy lobby.

Brenda hates the rain. She feels threatened by the
sound of heavy drops smacking onto the concrete. At the
same time, she feels it is too much information to lay on
a stranger.

Brenda: *I suppose it is good for the crops.*

Alice: *That's true. It's almost corn season. I can't
wait.*

Good conversation goes back and forth like a ten-
nis match. Alice receives Brenda's serve and volleys it
back with power for Brenda to hit. She considers food a
safe topic.

Brenda: *There's nothing like corn fresh from the
farm stand. Just pop it in the microwave for a few
minutes.*

Alice: *We like to grill ours outdoors.*

Brenda pays attention to the details in Alice's response. She reflects that this person used "we" and spoke
of outdoors which implies a family and a house. It feels
good to know something about this person. Brenda could
have offered that she lived alone in an apartment, but it
seems a dead end.

Emboldened by this bit of insight, Brenda feels
ready to move on. So far the participants have been responding to each other in I-statements, that is, statements
about themselves.

Brenda: *I really like your purse.*

Even though the statement begins with "I," it shifts the attention to Alice. It is essentially a you-statement.

Alice: *Oh, thank you. I found it at Macy's basement.*

Alice feels good about the compliment. She is more comfortable and expands on her answer.

Brenda also feels warmer and is willing to risk a question.

Brenda: *Do you shop there often?*

Clearly a you-statement. Good dialogue has some of each as participants share themselves to each other.

Alice: *It's the first place I look.*

The elevator dings, and the doors open. Half a dozen people emerge, and the people waiting step on. A man covers the control panel and asks for floors.

As Brenda gets off at 7, Alice says, "Have a nice day." Brenda responds in kind. They both feel a brief uplift from the momentary contact with another person. You don't have to talk about anything specific to make a connection.

Review. We look again at some of the conversation lessons of this dialogue:

- o Find an opener.
- o Speak slowly and distinctly and loud enough to be heard.
- o Use meaningful words ("purse" not "that thing") but not arcane words used to grab attention.
- o Avoid negativity.
- o Keep to safe topics until you feel some familiarity with the person.
- o Reciprocate.
- o Offer self-disclosure but only when appropriate.

o Use a mix of I-statements ("I like the weather"), you-statements ("you seem ready for the weather") and neutral statements ("it is good for the crops").
o Compliment when appropriate.
o Ask related questions, but avoid prying especially early in a relationship.

A random conversation can have a positive impact on a person's day.

First encounter. In a preliminary dialogue, you may meet someone you will encounter again, a new neighbor, a new person at a social gathering. At first you use polite conversation. The relationship will deepen over time or not, but you want to appear friendly at the outset.

Maintain good eye contact and positive body language, not too stiff or too slumped, not too encroaching or too defensive. Feel free to gesture with your hands as you talk, but keep them, as well as your face, in your own air space.

Speak respectfully of others, whether acquaintances or public figures, until you know more about this person's inclinations. Don't put down persons who may be his heroes.

Bonding. If you have a conversation with a person that you expect to talk to again, whether for the first time or the hundredth time, you lay the groundwork for future bonding. Gradually you share more about yourselves and get to know each other better. When you meet next, you can ask, "How's the cat?" At some point you may want to exchange phone numbers or email addresses as a commitment to continue.

Structure. Like an essay, a conversation often has an informal structure of opener, content, and conclusion.

Opener:

Greg: *Hi, Sam. It's good to see you. How have you been?*

Sam: *Pretty good. And yourself?*

Content: Either party can introduce a new topic.

Greg: *Not so good. My cat died.*

Sam: *I'm sorry to hear that. Did you have her long?*

When one topic is exhausted, either party can introduce a new topic.

Sam: *How about them Wolverines?*

Greg: *Phenomenal. They really pummeled Ohio State.*

Sam: *That interception in the second quarter was key.*

Conclusion: Either party may move to conclude the conversation.

Greg: *Well, I've got to get going. Been good seeing you again.*

Sam: *Yeah, been great. We'll have to do it again.*

When the conversation follows a structure, each person knows his role at any point in the conversation. It makes it easy to come up with the right response.

Openers. The question is how to start. You want to start with a topic that is familiar and easy for the other person to respond to. Some examples would be:

o The weather. A tried and true opener, it has the misfortune of being exhausted quickly. Either it is a nice day or not. You can follow up by asking if the other person has any plans for such a nice (or snowy) day.

o Mutual acquaintances. Positive comments on family and friends, or the people that brought you together in this environment.

o Health. Questions about health demonstrate compassion.
o Current affairs including the environment. Carefully. Your meaningful discussions can be with those
   who know you better.
o Sports. Even when people support opposing teams,
   the conversation has a good-natured give and take.
o Books.
o Cooking.
o Entertainment.
o Gardening and landscaping.
o Art in the broadest sense. The new museum exhi-
   bition, special celebrations (the state bicentennial),
   jazz in the park on summer evenings.
o Travel.
o Technologies (including cell phone, smart home
   with computer-operated things).
o Happenings in your neighborhood/building.
o Classes and hobbies. (Draw on your activities as
   listed in chapters 7-9.)
   Ask specific questions.
o Tell me about you. (This almost sounds like a
   pick-up line. Use it carefully in situations where
   genuine interest is appropriate.)
o What do you do? How is it going?
o How has your week been? Anything exciting happen?
o Any plans for the weekend?
o At a restaurant: It all looks yummy. What looks
   good to you?
o At a social setting: How do you know the
   host/hostess/deceased?
o At the senior center: What days do you usually
   come?

Any of these openers can be used mid-conversation when energy for the current topic has been exhausted.

Content. Share the time. Your ideas are good and need to be stated, but do not expound on them until the other person has had a chance to comment. If the other person has a tendency to dominate the conversation, make a small comments like "I see," or "You don't say" to show you are paying attention. At a pause, be ready to interject "Well, the way I see it is" and add your comments. The other person probably doesn't mean to dominate the conversation but needs your help to avoid doing so. Otherwise he goes home with no new input other than repeating his own ideas.

Remain interested. If your attention starts to wander, bring it back as in meditation. Listen to what is being said rather than focusing on what you will say. If a lull comes, you can look at how you will advance the conversation at your turn.

If the conversation dies, look for threads that were put out but not pursued earlier. She says, "I moved to Iowa the year my brother died, and I started working for the company immediately." She then goes on about her career with the company. When she seems to have finished with that topic, you can follow with, "Was your brother your only sibling?" She had mentioned him, and it is not prying to go back to him. You can also expand on the topic of Iowa by saying what you like about living there. If there seems nowhere to go, refer back to that pocket of openers you have stashed in your brain and start a new topic. Also you could move to the conclusion.

Ending. You don't need an excuse to end the conversation, and many excuses sound weak. Avoid being abrupt or leaving when the speaker is mid-sentence.

When a lull occurs simply say, "It's been good talking to you. I've enjoyed it." Your counterpart may have similar ideas and respond in kind. "You take care."

If the speaker launches into another story, decide how firm you need to be. Continue moving toward the conclusion, trying to hit the middle between urgency and patience. Extricate yourself gracefully.

Problems. We all have issues—health, finances, relationships—you name it. Because of the pressure, the trouble wants to be the first thing that comes out of your mouth, but is that appropriate? It will kidnap the conversation, rendering everything else irrelevant in comparison.

Can you bring up a personal problem? Do you have a deep enough level of bonding with this person? Otherwise you are making your complaints a focal point of the meeting with no purpose other than to air them. Concentrate on a different topic and get the satisfaction of some temporary distraction, an opportunity to relate to a person on a different level.

For example, your assisted living facility is raising its rates and you can no longer afford it. Meanwhile your sister-in-law stops by to bring you books she is discarding. Is it fair to unload on her about the rent? She doesn't know you well enough to consider the options. She might think you're going to hit on your brother. Talk about the books with her, and leave the quandary for others in the building facing the same rent increase or for the social worker.

Empathy. On the other hand, the other person may bring up a problem. To offer empathy is to go beyond the facts to see the significance they have for the person speaking. Try to feel what she is feeling. Has she made herself vulnerable to you, or is she protecting herself? If vulnerable, you want to validate her feelings and perhaps share some of your own. If protective, you want for her to feel safe. Let her feel that you can be trusted by looking her in the eye, perhaps touching her arm.

Alice: *I don't know what to do about my job.*

This is not the place to change the topic. Follow through with a you-statement.

Brenda: *You've said you were thinking of leaving.*

Alice: *I don't know where to go.*

If you have any helpful information, you can offer it.

Brenda: *I hear Christ Hospital is hiring.*

Do not offer advice.

[NOT} Brenda: *I think you should stay where you are.*

It is not your responsibility to problem-solve.

[NOT] Brenda: *Check the newspaper.*

Offer support without taking over.

Brenda: *A transition like that is tough. Is there anything I can do?*

You imagine what the situation must feel like for her. Is she facing loss of income, loss of position, or other problems? What does she need from you? You cannot fix the situation, but you can offer to be there for her as she straightens it out.

Disagreement. Unlike a debate, a conversation does not seek to score points or win an argument. Even though you may disagree with the main premise, you can try to find points to agree on.

Alice: *The Beatles weren't the same after Paul died.*

[NOT] Brenda: *That's so ridiculous. Everybody knows that was just a stupid story that got started. Sir Paul is alive and well and on concert tour this summer.*

[NOT] Alice: *Haven't you heard "Walrus?" I am not ridiculous.*

[NOT] Brenda: *You are if that's what you believe.*

This is not a happy conversation. Neither one will go home feeling good. They might try instead:

Alice: *The Beatles weren't the same after Paul died.*

Brenda: *I was never convinced that Paul had died, but I agree that some of their later albums didn't have the power of earlier ones.*

Alice: *Like the song "Drive My Car." Neither the melody nor the words measure up.*

It's not necessary to refute an issue head-on. While you might not want to appear to be in agreement with the basic premise, you can find ways to pull the conversation together. You do not have to cede your position. If the speaker crosses the line and makes a strong statement contrary to the views you have expressed, you can say, "I'll think more about that." It's the old saying agree to disagree.

Speaker's block. As in writer's block, the right word isn't there; the relevant phrase doesn't manifest itself. Your mind whirrs in neutral gear. Nothing comes out.

I have to admit that I am not glib, not one of those people who can open their mouths and have the right thing to say. I have to pay attention to a conversation and be ready to follow its flow, like painting a wall. Follow up on what was just said. "That must have felt cold." Or contribute from your own experience. "I was once so cold."

You have something to offer to a conversation. Sometimes you have to collect yourself to find what it is. Remember that the purpose is not to appear witty or learned but to give to the other person. A sincere remark suffices. Intent more than content distinguishes a real conversation.

One technique to get out of a block is to repeat what the speaker just said.

Alice: *One good song from that period was "Yesterday."*

Brenda: *Yeah, I really liked "Yesterday."*

Another technique is to have in your mind emergency topics to draw on when you get stuck. Introduce this new topic.

Brenda: *Say, did you see that new movie?*

Alice: *Yeah, that was great.*

Brenda: *I liked the scene…*

As she had left her apartment that morning, Brenda had stopped and asked herself what was on her repertoire of possible topics. The movie came to mind, as did the need to give the new employee further training. She would use that with her supervisor.

If she knew whom she was going to encounter, she could reflect about them and come up with a pertinent topic.

Brenda: *How does your shoulder feel after the surgery?*

Remember your lessons on self-esteem. Don't listen to the negative doubts. "Whatever I say is stupid." Have the confidence to open your mouth and give affirmation to the other person.

Afterwards. Reflect back on what points might have been left on the table for a later time. The cardiologist? It's okay that it wasn't addressed this time. The conversation didn't move in that direction. Like the mighty Mississippi, it flows where it will.

Don't let your overview become a self-evaluation.
I *could* have said this. I *should* have said that. Just as you
gave to your partner, now give to yourself the joy of having connected.

Courage. Be brave and try to converse with someone. What is the worst that could happen? I suppose you
could make a social *faux pas*, say something out of left
field, but what if you do?

You could go out in the garden on a fine day.
What's the worst that could happen? I suppose you could
get stung by a honeybee. But that is an infrequent occur-
rence. It would be a shame to give up the riotous colors
of the zinnias for fear of that small chance. And if the bee
does sting you, the pain will dissipate over time and you
will also have the memory of the zinnias.

Similarly for the inappropriate remark. It stings at
first. You are judging yourself again. But over time you
forget the pain and you have memory of the conversation.

Give. Consider yourself a cafeteria worker whose
responsibility it is to put new salads on the line to keep it
stocked. If you stand back and watch as people go by, the
line will be diminished for lack of food. If you make up
your mind to give, to be attentive to the needs of the people coming through, you will help create a satisfying
meal experience for them and a good day for you. Conversation is about generosity. Make it your mindset.

Challenge for Change. Think of at least three topics you could use in a conversation.

18. Friendship

Don't walk in front of me… I may not follow
Don't walk behind me… I may not lead
Walk beside me… just be my friend
Albert Camus

Definition. Friendship touches the soul. Two or more voices harmonize together in ways that no voice alone can achieve. Simply defined, a friend feels good to be with. Souls soothe out the rough edges for each other. The ideas that rattle loose in your head have somewhere to go to be connected. The feelings, the expressions of hope and despair, joy and sorrow, all resonate with each other. The soul feels more complete.

A friend understands, or tries to, gives affection freely, aligns her feelings with your experiences of good or bad, holds your trust and does not betray you. She is honest but doesn't judge.

A friend is a strong positive experience when you encounter him, as you are for him. You seek him out because he stimulates you with frequent conversation or communication. He knows how your mind works. You laugh with a friend and mourn with him, try out new ideas on him, and sometimes enjoy silence with him. If possible you do things with your friend, share experiences, build memories, so that your friendship has a mutual history.

Where would Tom Sawyer be without Huck Finn? When they saw a man killed, they swore to each other they would not tell for fear of reprisal. They shared a common concept of how such oaths ought to be taken. Tom wrote it out, and, by pricking their fingers with a needle, they signed the oath that Tom had written in blood:

Huck Finn and
Tom Sawyer swears
they will keep mum
about This and They
wish They may Drop
down dead in Their
Tracks if They ever
Tell and Rot.

Mark Twain, *The Adventures of Tom Sawyer*, Chapter X.

Commonality. Through their common life experiences, Tom and Huck arrived at the appropriate way to handle an oath of secrecy. You often share a similar outlook with a friend, which is not to say you agree on everything. I had a friend with whom I shared a fundamental values system, but our expression of it in the political arena was diametrically opposed. At times he made a kidding remark about "that President that I had elected," and I would respond in the same vein. Having acknowledged our differences, we left it there. We didn't argue the issues. We had established our individual rights to our opinions and moved on.

Generally, but not always, the more you have in common in terms of life experiences, values, place in life, the tighter the bond will be, like gluing a broken china cup whose pieces fit well together. At the same time, each of you wants to bring something new to the relationship so that you can compare notes on life. You might both work in finance, but she is black and you are white, equals but with different experiences.

A friend helps another to hold to higher principles. You are angry at some situation and want revenge. Your friend listens, sympathizes. Yes, she can see you are angry; yes, the anger is justified. But the need for revenge is poisonous to the soul and might create further harm to you. What other ways might that anger be dealt with? The friend brings out the good in you.

A. C. Grayling says, "...we value autonomy, self-determination, and the construction and enhancements of a personal identity as very high goods in themselves. To honor these things in another is to be a friend to that other. To respect the autonomy of another, her right to the final say on important decisions and choices, is to be a good friend to her."[10]

You may have common interests, like cooking or reading certain books or traveling or studying the Civil War. When you converse, you can draw on these topics. They provide a backdrop for the other exigencies of life.

Where would Lucy be without Ethel? They lived in the same apartment building, were both married, and shared similar outlooks. Ethel had recently had a disagreement with Fred, and she knew how her friend felt when Lucy and Ricky weren't talking.

Ethel tries to encourage Lucy to call Ricky. Lucy insists that he has to call first.

Ethel: *What if he never calls you?*

Lucy: *Then we will just never see each other.*

Ethel: *Oh, we can't have that. Now let's see.*

Trying to think of a solution for her best friend, Ethel bandages Lucy to look like she was hit by a bus so as to gain Ricky's sympathy.

---

[10] Grayling, A.C., *Friendship*, p. 182.

"Fred and Ethel Fight," *I Love Lucy*, S1 E22, March 10, 1952.

This type of zany adventure is typical of their relationship. Perhaps it reminds you of a friendship you may have known.

Another perspective. My friend Lee recently wrote:

> Too many students were admitted to the University of Michigan in 1965 - there was no place to put them all. There was a scramble to find lecture halls large enough to hold everyone. In the residence halls, single rooms were turned into doubles, doubles into triples. There were even bunk beds set up in the basements. I lived in South Quad, in one of those doubles-turned-triples, so I had two room-mates to adjust to.

> My first room-mate, Janet-from-New-York, had arrived a few days earlier and was already bored. The second one, Marty, also from New York, arrived after me and was thrilled about everything, and most of all thrilled that I had not claimed the lower bunk (Janet had already snagged the single bed). They hated each other; I kept out of the way.

> The smart money would have been on Janet, but she ended up moving next door, into what became a quadruple, and I was stuck with Marty. I didn't like her much, but it did make life simpler.

> So that was how I met my best friend. And I couldn't tell you when exactly she became a friend instead of a room-mate, but I do remember my mother saying (later on that semester), "But I thought you didn't like her!" and me being sur-

prised. At that point it felt like we had always been not only friends but good friends. It was a case, I guess, where life - just living it, every day - turns acquaintances into friends. This doesn't always happen, but Marty is easy to get along with, never critical and never demanding, always supportive and always willing to join in whatever fun is going around. And she still finds life thrilling. So we remain friends, even though she doesn't write and I don't phone.

Attendance. Sharing afflictions as they arise occurs in friendship, but the relationship does not dwell on those or it withers. The goal is not to seek to be consoled so much as to engage in life. Although bad times need support, the strength of the relationship comes in building on the positive.

At the core is attendance. A friendship cannot be maintained without mutual effort to connect regularly in some form.

You may have a mutual history with some friends, may have been college roommates or high school or even grade school chums. By attending to the old relationships, you maintain them. New friendships may arise throughout your lifetime, but only those precious old friends can reminisce with you. We enter into the crisis of loneliness when those friends go away or pass away.

Personal experience. In the first forty years of my life, I moved fourteen times, or roughly once every three years child and adult, all but one of them interstate. I never had a chance at developing intimacies, never even learned how.

My own periods of friendship have varied. Usually an elementary school chum accompanied me at recess,

and kids in my neighborhood came around. In high
school I ran with a group of dateless girls, going to
games together and playing bridge.

I settled and raised a family. When I lived in Con-
necticut, I served on a whirlwind of various organizations. I took the kids to the community pool and always
knew several mothers to converse with poolside. I felt
proud of being so connected.

By the time we moved to Massachusetts, I was
burned out. Besides we had our own backyard pool. I
kept to myself and knew no one. Each year on the first
day of school, the mothers gathered on the street corner
to wait with the kids for the bus. I wondered how the two
across the street knew each other so well. I had never
seen them crossing the lawns to visit. Was there a proto-
col? Or did they just drop in? My mother never dropped
in, knew her neighbors only slightly, and so did I.

Reciprocity. Most friendships have some degree
of reciprocity, of exchange of initiative or small kind-
nesses. You may bring back a souvenir from a trip for a
friend, or she may drive you to an appointment. Rarely is
there a strict accountability of tit-for-tat and this-for-that,
and such a compulsive exchange may be harmful to the
friendship. Similarly you share your support for each
other. One time you provide the empathy and compassion
to your friend's negative experiences, and at another time
(maybe even on the same day) she is the source of support for you.

As a mutual feeling, generosity dictates that sometimes one person will make the magnanimous gesture to
another. It is not so much returned the following Tuesday
as it is held in the mutual memory of the friends. Should
the need ever arise for either of them, a similar gesture
will be there without question.

Where would David (who killed Goliath) be without Jonathan? When David feared that Jonathan's father King Saul would try to take David's life, Jonathan said, "I will sound out my father about this time tomorrow. Whether he is well disposed toward David or not, I will send you the information."

Jonathan learned that his father was indeed murderously angry toward David, and Jonathan warned his friend to go away. They departed in tears swearing the Lord "shall be between you and me, and between your posterity and mine forever."

New American Bible, 1 Samuel 20:12, 42

Disparate relationships. Friends are not always equals. Sometimes one is the more dominant with ideas on what to do next while the other is more a follower. Sometimes one is the expert who comes over to show you how to make pineapple upside-down cake. So long as it works for both of you, it can be beneficial.

Where would Frodo be without Sam? Frodo agreed to take the Ring, and Elrond Half-elven conceded that it was a heavy burden.

Sam: *But you won't send him off alone, surely, Master?*

Elrond: *You at least shall go with him. It is hardly possible to separate you from him even when he is summoned to a secret council and you are not.*

J. R. R. Tolkien, *The Lord of the Rings.*

At the end, when Sam carried Frodo up the mountain and the Ring had been dropped into the Cracks of Doom, the earth shuddered and toppled. Great cracks opened up from it and fire belched from them. It looked like the end for the hobbits.

Frodo: *I am glad you are here with me. Here at the end of all things, Sam*

J.R.R. Tolkien, *The Lord of the Rings.*

But it was not the end of all things, and they returned to the Shire..

Caution. Some relationships are not beneficial to you and should be avoided. A person who purports to be your friend may attempt to separate you from other friends by criticizing them, running them down, or portraying them as not quite acceptable. You have to ask yourself who is actually the negative influence in your life.

Sometimes an exploitative person borrows money without returning it or stands you up on a regular basis. You want to cull such toxic relationships from your life.

On the other hand, more friendships end due to misunderstandings and hurt feelings than from a lack of commonality. If you are peeved at someone who in general has been a good friend to you, try to find a way to normalize the relationship, even if it means bending a bit.

The *Golden Girls* were a circle of three friends, actually roommates. On one occasion, Dorothy had been insensitive to Blanche and Rose. When she realized it, she asked,

Dorothy: *Can you ever forgive me?*

Blanche: *Should we give her another chance?*

Rose: *We'd better. Best friends are hard to come by.*

Golden Girls, S03 E15

Mutual commitment. In friendships there is a mutual commitment to the happiness of the other. A person does not ask a friend to compromise their principles. Rather he is a good influence on the friend's life. You want to guard against only being drawn to friends who are physically attractive. We come in all shapes and sizes with all manner of noses and chins.

I settled down and lived in Cincinnati for over two decades. I had friends then, some close who were with me for most of that time, others whose company I enjoyed when it happened.

I moved again four years ago and keep up with the Ohio friends only by email or phone. I have people here whom I would consider friends, but I have known them fewer than two years, been close enough to pick up the phone less than that. Yes, there have been times when I have been lonely, but I have been able to reach out.

Circle of friends. Many elderly often say they prefer a network of connections. They may have lost the all-important connection with a significant other, and to start down the road to replacement is too involved and too risky. Instead they prefer a small circle of friends, persons they call on almost equally. If you enter into old age with such a circle intact, you have an advantage, but you can always begin to add to a circle with dedicated effort. The next chapter discusses this.

Epidemic. It has become a cliché to speak of the "loneliness epidemic" in popular books and magazines. The percent of people who report they feel lonely for a measurable amount of time has increased over the past decades. The culture is not as receptive to the idea of making friends.

Some people are burned out on the effort of trying to make friends and prefer to live a solitary life. They feel a sense of shame surrounding their loneliness as if it were their fault, when in fact the culture is to blame. Having felt rejected previously, the lonely person reacts in a more hostile manner to attempts to engage him, thus perpetuating his loneliness. "Unchecked loneliness fuels continued loneliness by keeping us afraid to reach out."[11]

If you know such a person, and we all do, the best you can do is to maintain a positive attitude. Greet him with "Good morning" without demanding a response. In time he may come to acknowledge you, not to trust you because that's too much to ask, but to be open to your presence. I have seen such a person open out gradually over a year of acknowledging him, and it was a treasure to see him smile a little.

Fear of rejection. As we age, fewer of us drive. We can't get around to each other like we did. If we live long enough, friends eventually go away (as I did), or others move to a facility, or pass away.

Fear of rejection keeps us from reaching out. The city operates a van service for disabled: a vehicle with half a dozen seats in two rows and space next to the driver for walkers. Sometimes when I board the van another passenger sits there. We greet each other, but then we ride in silence, missing the opportunity to connect with another human being. Even though I know I shouldn't, I let my fears of being inappropriate inhibit me.

The whole world needs to be braver. People need to be willing to take the risk to be more vulnerable with others. It may not always work out, but sometimes we will find a spark of affinity, and a relationship will be born. If not we shake the dust off our feet and move on to the next encounter. We will in time find a person who is hungry for what we have to offer.

It goes back to the issue of self-esteem (see chapter 4). You find yourself listening to the negative thoughts, the self-doubts, the thoughts of not good enough. Chal-

[11] Brown, Brené, *Braving the Wilderness*, Random House, New York, 2017.

lenge those thoughts. Not good enough for what? To talk to another human being? You have something to offer.

Turn your mind to the other person. Think in terms of giving to her—a warm voice, acknowledgement of her as a person. All she needs is some encouragement. We human beings are funny creatures with tough exteriors like a crab but an interior that is soft and eager to be touched.

Affection. Physical touch is often part of affection. The skin is considered a bodily organ just like the heart or the liver, but as the largest bodily organ it is external. It feels touch, pressure, pain, cold, warmth. Consider the sudden shock to your whole system when you skinned your knee as a kid.

Physical affection has to be appropriate and wanted. Recall the welcome feeling of a warm hug, the creeped-out feeling of an unwanted touch. We have to know the other person's proclivities. Often as friends we communicate through the sense of touch, a hand on the shoulder, a handshake, a high-five, a pat on the head.

Reassurance. Friends reassure each other. Where would Winnie the Pooh be without Piglet?

Pooh: *I don't feel very much like Pooh today.*

Piglet: *There, there. I'll bring you tea and honey until you do.*

A.A. Milne, *Winnie-the-Pooh*

Perhaps you don't at the moment have a Piglet in your life. This society can feel closed, but it has its openings. Don't give up. Be open. Your life will feel more fruitful if you allow yourself to be touched by others however incidentally.

And the friendship ends. Frodo and Sam waited as the travelers came forward, the leaders of the elves and Bilbo.

Bilbo: *Are you coming?*

Sam: *Where are you going?*

Frodo: *To the Havens, Sam.*

Sam: *And I can't come?*

Frodo: *No, Sam. Do not be too sad, Sam, You cannot always be torn in two. You will have to be one and whole, for many years. You have so much to enjoy and to be and to do.*

J.R.R. Tolkien, *The Lord of the Rings.*

In the end we have to overcome our loneliness. We have to continue to reach out in big gestures and small. We have to adjust our expectations and learn to be content with what life brings. You have so much to enjoy and to be and to do.

Challenge for Change. Acknowledge someone. It can be a phone call to an old friend you haven't heard from recently or a shy "Hi" to a stranger in the elevator. Open the door.

19. Making Friends

If you build it, they will come.
Field of Dreams, 1989.

Availability. On occasion friends grow on trees and are there for the asking, but often you have to seek them out. As the lifestyles of elderly people evolve, they no longer have as many opportunities to form casual friendships. Gone are the colleagues at work, the parents of the kids' friends at soccer matches, neighbors who cross the lawn.

In order to establish friendships, you have to be more proactive. You engage with people you come across at senior centers, church potlucks, or residential facilities. You move beyond initial pleasantries to establishing an ongoing relationship.

Build a friendship. You now have all the skills you need—self-confidence, conversational starters, and compassion. You only need to offer these to people who are lonely for them. Offer a place for friendship, and some will follow.

"If you build it." What is "It?"

A place for friendship. Imagine a place for friendship to thrive, not a physical place but a spiritual place. A person approaching this place would feel safe, would feel wanted. If you build such a place, people would come. You present to others that you are possible as a friend.

What do people look for in a friend? If you express an interest in someone's positive qualities, she will feel valued. You accept her ideas as part of her being even if you don't agree with them. Between you and her, you are building a place that feels comfortable for friendship to exist, one that is based on trust and camaraderie.

Loyalty. A person feels safe when she is respected and appreciated. The space you are building is weather-proof. Even when you are not present to each other, you don't mock her to others. In high school I had a friend who was different, not caught up in teen fads, and didn't fit in. I enjoyed her company.

When I was with another group of friends, they ridiculed her behind her back, the way she dressed, the way she talked. When it came time to put in my two cents, I said, 'I like her." They couldn't argue that simple statement of fact. It deflected all of their observations, and the topic was dropped. A friend has to be loyal, not go with the crowd. Likewise, your friend's secrets have to be safe with you.

Field of dreams. If you are building such a space, another person may become intrigued by the idea of friendship Picture the final scene of *Field of Dreams* if you saw it. In the dusky Iowa countryside, a parade of headlights appears, all headed to the field of dreams. If you build it, they will come. As the young daughter in the movie says, people are drawn to it without knowing why. The pacifist author adds, "They'll come to Iowa for reasons they can't even fathom. ... They'll come to your door. ... It'll be as if they dipped themselves in magic water." Similarly some will be attracted to your field of dreams, the friendship you are offering, and will want to explore it further.

An unreserved person will be clear in their efforts to get to know you, but what of the timid person? She may have felt rejected in previous attempts to start a friendship. Her response may be more subtle, more protective of self, but you can discern it if you are watching.

Tree house. The Little Rascals had their tree house, a place to gather, plan adventure, and recall adventure. Although you are not planning a physical structure, you want your offered friendship to be just as tangible. It must be specific. "Yes, I want you to be my friend." You do that by initiating conversations, exchanging numbers, making plans to meet.

The friendship you are offering to build has to be desirable to the other person. You offer warmth, sincerity, a place for openness. Even with all of this, some will not want what you are offering. It's not to their taste; that's okay. Maybe your tree house is in an oak tree, and they want maple. You promise to part amicably and look further. The world is a lonely enough place that you will find someone for whom your friendship is desirable.

Reciprocity. Consider the possibility that someone is building for you a space for a friendship to exist. Are you paying attention? Do you notice the ladder to the tree house? Be ready to offer reciprocity.

I try to change my life patterns to bring them more in accord with what is expected of people who wish to engage. Is it manipulative? We are not talking about catching and toasting toads. I am offering myself to coexist alongside with other people, not controlling or seducing them. If the offer of my person is something they want, then they can accept it. If not, we both move on from there.

"They will come." Who are "They?"

I am hoping for some friends. Among the people I know, whom am I drawn to?

Is this someone I can love, because that is what friendship is all about? Realistically there are few that I can't love if I put my heart to it. I can't see myself seeking friendship with someone who is cruel and malicious. Other than that, my heart is open to anyone. So he drools a little bit. It's probably the meds. He talks to me about places I've never been, sometimes the same story twice in one day. That's okay, too.

I draw concentric circles and place my contacts within them, the closer persons in the smaller central circles expanding out to people less well known in the larger.

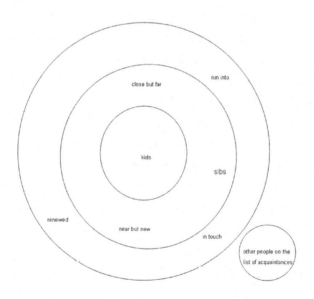

Adult children. The kids are in my center circle as being the persons to whom I am closest. They are the only ones. Many people my age experience this.

The middle child is nearby (forty miles). None are in the same town. I am self-sufficient but lonely. They see me as elderly now, not on the same level as them, perhaps not to be trusted to stay out of trouble. The one who is closest comes up with his wife every few weeks to change overhead light bulbs and take me out to dinner. I appreciate that. The kids are nearest and dearest to my heart, but they project that they have their own lives. The grandkids are all thousands of miles away.

Close people. The next circle has sibs, one older, two younger, all also thousands of miles away. We communicate mostly by phone and internet. We don't travel as much as we used to. I feel comfortable with them, feel up-to-date with the major aspects of their lives. We have no standing feuds. I need to make the effort to contact them more often.

Also in that circle are "close but far," that is, people with whom I once felt close but who are now distant geographically. That was my fault. I moved. Again phone and internet have to suffice. I have no doubt that if we were to sit down to lunch again, we would resume where we left off with no distance, no awkwardness of time between us.

The "near but new" people I have met in the past couple of years. I like them and consider them friends, but we have but a brief history together. Most of them know each other. We have the advantage of being able to relax together for a prolonged conversation on occasion.

Next circle. I have renewed a couple of old friendships (high school and college) in the past couple of years. I enjoy learning what these people are doing now, where we have followed similar paths and where divergent ones. They too are friends.

Some people I keep loosely in touch with, every two or three months. We mostly just catch up on the news, whose kid was married, who is getting physical therapy. Extended family like cousins is mostly on the Christmas card list. I am interested in them but never seem to communicate otherwise.

Be open to adding names to the outer circles. What about the woman on the back seat of the van? Ask her if she's having a good day. She may answer tersely, but she might spark a conversation. The encounter may not blossom into a friendship, but it does count for human contact. She has ceased to be the woman in the back and has become Stella whose son is visiting from Vermont.

Attention. I can get even more out of the contacts with the people in my circles by pursuing them more assertively (not aggressively). For instance, I can make the effort to follow up with "near but new" more consistently. If I haven't heard from someone, then it is time for me to get in touch. I find that as often as not I have been the one to let the communications ball drop.

Promote from within. If a person has been in circle 3, promote them to circle 2 with more frequent contact. I can share more of my life with them to make it more interesting, and I can ask more about what is going on with them to give them the opportunity to share.

Feuds. Sometimes we are disconnected from people in our circles, especially family members, because of some long-standing disagreement. Nobody quite remembers the original issues. Make an effort to reconcile. Whatever the cause (especially money), it is not as important now as the loss of connection.

Suggest to the person letting the past go. Possibly a third party can mediate an open discussion to make sure it doesn't evolve into blame. Each name on your circle is worth salvaging. Let go.

Dunbar's number. An evolutionary psychologist Dr. Robin Dunbar from Oxford University in the U.K. has done some research on our circles of friends. According to him, they are distributed as follows:

5 very close friends

10 close friends

35 friends

100 acquaintances

That brings the number to 150, which is the maximum number of acquaintances one person can realistically keep within their social network because of the structure of the neocortex. This is known as Dunbar's number.[12]

I listed my acquaintances, counting anyone at all whom I would expect to know me by name. My list totaled 90, yet I am satisfied with it as being a nice list. Again there is the possibility of reaching out to someone on the list but not on the diagram and adding them to an outer circle, maybe to be moved in further as time goes on.

The process. In reaching out more to people, I find my life is fuller. I feel more surrounded by people. The gaps in the day don't feel as frustrating. I make more effort to notice the needs of the people around me. I give them my attention, and with it I give them my love. They will come.

---

[12] Leaver, Kate, *op. cit.*, p. 23.

You have something to offer. My kids grew up on Mr. Rogers. As he would say, you are special. Ask someone, "Please won't you be my neighbor?"

Challenge for Change. Draw concentric circles and map out the important people in your life. Look to see who you have been neglecting. How could you be loving them better? Pick up the phone.

20. Telecommunication

In this experiment, made on the 9th of October, 1876, actual conversation, backwards and forwards, upon the same line, and by the same instruments reciprocally used, was successfully carried on for the first time upon a real line of miles in length.
Alexander Graham Bell

Loneliness. The score is 11-3 in the fifth inning. Whether backing the winning team or the losing, this game is done. Stick it with a fork. That leaves the rest of the evening to get through, and you are alone.

For whatever reason you can't get out to mingle with humanity. You may experience being alone as a sharp pain or a dull ache. Using imaging technique to examine how the brain processes pain, it has been demonstrated that experiences such a loneliness and social exclusion literally hurt in the same process as physical pain.[13]. Mostly you experience it as a too-often feeling, a habit of emptiness, a helplessness of despair.

Yet the phone lines are humming with calls between friends and relatives and business associates. The very air waves around you are brimming with electronic messages. You only need to reach out and to pull them down.

Telecommunication means communicating across a distance (*tele-*). If you read Victorian novels, you find that they were frequently sending written messages physically across town through a servant or postman who car-

---

[13] Floyd, Ph.D., Kory, *The Loneliness Cure*, p. 125.

ried them. ("Can you come for tea today?" "My daughter is not interested in your proposal." "We must postpone the sale of the estate.") Now using new devices, we can tap into each other's world across the miles and around the globe.

Telephone. Although the telephone was first invented 150 years ago, many forms of communication have only existed for thirty years or less. As the number of elderly people has increased, so has the number of ways to break through the silence. When face-to-face contact is not feasible, the opportunity of a phone call comes in a close second. You can hear the voice and its inflections. You respond to each other in real time. The reassurance of simultaneous laughter beats "LOL" (Laughing Out Loud).

The phone can provide lovely experiences if you remember that you own it; it doesn't own you. See its ring as an invitation to move outside of yourself. If you have friends who call too early or too late, let them know your preferences and allow the call to go to voice mail.

Occasionally the call can be from a salesperson. You can break in with, "I'm not interested," and hang up. You don't have to wait for him to draw a breath because he never will.

Calls come without distinctions from either cell phone or landline. Some people don't pick up a ringing phone unless they know the name shown on caller ID. Instead they let it go to voice mail. That adds another step in the communication process, but it is a personal preference to avoid the machine-originated robocalls. At some point someone has to identify themselves.

Often the call will be from somebody you are happy to connect with. Follow the same tendencies as for any conversation, some give, some take, some listening, some talk about them, some talk about you. Relax and enjoy the encounter in a sharing environment.

For any given call, the amount of time you talk depends on the person and their needs. I talk longer with my sisters and my kids. With some people at some times we don't have as much to say. Even good friends may be calling just to convey a specific message.

Once the primary exchange of news and views has taken place, once the flow of talk has become loose rambling, you can end the conversation if you choose. "It's been good talking to you, but I have to go now." Go where? You don't need to come up with an excuse. When it is time for you to get off the phone, that in itself is reason enough without creating a story. The kitchen is on fire. My grandkid just fell off the swing. The plants are dying.

Remember that a phone call may be a gift to another. When you are planning what to do in some part of the day, consider that someone might actually like to hear from you, that you can be an enhancement to their lonely time, that you might bring a smile to their face, unseen but heard through the phone wires.

Disclaimer. I have arbitrarily divided readers into three groups of people:

- o 1. Modern technology fascinates the first group, and they use its various platforms to communicate. They could have written this chapter. The have nothing to gain by reading it and can skip ahead to Chapter 21.
- o 2. Alternate forms of communication bore if not frighten the second group. They dismiss the topic altogether by saying they are not interested, that they like things the way they are. This group also has nothing to gain from this chapter because it is

information they don't want. Move on to Chapter 21.

- o 3, The third group has heard about telecommunication devices but never had the opportunity to explore them. They suspect that such devices have the capacity to ease them out of their loneliness. This chapter will perhaps help them find a way to get started.

Reading the chapter is like logging onto amazon.com. It tells you what is out there in thumbnail sketches, but you can't know what it's like until you try it for yourself.

Email (electronic mail). Email has been around for decades, one of the early manifestations of the World Wide Web. Email involves sending and receiving written messages, but it does not have the immediacy of text messaging discussed later.

To send and receive email you must have a mailbox online which you get from a mailbox provider. For general purposes people often use one of the popular free providers such as yahoo.com or gmail.com, but you will see a wide variety of domain names in use. Any administrator of a registered domain name can be a provider.

When you open your mailbox, you will see any new messages. By clicking on a message you can open it to read it; you have the option to reply or forward. Usually you can send messages to any mailbox while only users can read or delete messages from their mailbox. Sometimes a business will send you a message from a "do not reply" mailbox which means nobody is monitoring the input.

Once sent, an email lives forever unless the receiver deletes it. If you make a promise, say to buy a car, that intent exists in writing. Be as careful as if you were sending a written document over your signature. Rather than typing, "I will buy the car" (a commitment). say, "I am considering buying the car" and withhold firm commitment until you have seen it.

The wrong message. Over the phone your voice conveys the underlying sentiment of your thought. In print such as email or text, the words by themselves can be misunderstood. Nothing indicates if you are kidding or teasing. If you express frustration, it comes across as reproval. Be very careful of the impact your words may have. At all times send a positive message.

Pay attention to the address line of your email. I once received a chatty email from my ex-husband's second wife. It turned out she had a friend with the same first name, and autofill selected the wrong address. Fortunately no family secrets were revealed.

Reciprocity. Just as in other facets of friendship, the principle of reciprocity underlies interaction through social media. Consider responding within a reasonable time to a first message from someone you know. Don't leave them hanging. After that you will have the option to keep the chain going for multiple subsequent messages.

You will also receive email from commercial enterprises. If you order flowers online, you will be on the flowers mailing list forever unless you go to the bottom of the email and click unsubscribe.

Caring. In all forms of communication, the object is to listen, reflect, and give. The same principles as for building friendships apply here. You want to create a safe space where the other person is appreciated.

Messaging. The term messaging can be a generic term used to indicate sending and receiving text messages on a cell phone or posting messages on such environments as Facebook and Twitter. It also can mean using a specific service such as Instant Messenger (IM). There has to be some interface.

Both sender and receiver must use the same software for a message to be readable. Businesses often message through specific programs particular to their industry.

The value of messaging lies in the fact that it is often a one-to-one correspondence similar to email but with more immediacy. You can use voice recognition software to speak your message directly into the phone or computer without having to type it. The device recognizes the words and turns them into type.

Cell phone. You may already have a cell phone. Wherever you go, you see people talking into and gazing at a cell phone. Four people in a restaurant booth will each be staring or poking at their individual cell phones. A mother walking her baby in a stroller will be pushing with one hand and holding the cell phone to her face with the other.

When asked which they touched quite a lot, people responded:

cell phone	57.2%
family member	28.6%
closest friend	16.7%[14]

Some of the uses of a cell phone:
○ telephone
○ text message
○ email
○ internet connection (including search and news feeds)
○ social media (such as Facebook)
○ camera
○ photo storage

---

[14] Floyd, *ibid.,* p. 54.

○ flashlight
○ games
○ apps from app store

Videophony (Skype). If you add pictures of the caller to the telephone experience, you have videophony. Most people think of Skype, but they are not synonymous. Other services also offer videophony, and Skype also offers other services besides videophony such as global telephone.

You download the videophony software you choose. You can get recommendations from people you know or search on the web. There may be a monthly fee or a fee per time used. Anticipate how you will use it to decide what the best deal is.

You can use desktop, laptop, or cell phone. Each caller must have a forward-facing camera mounted toward them. When the call is placed, you are able to see the image of the caller on your screen, and he can see your image on his screen. You converse as normal, but you are able to see a smile or a shrug of the shoulders. Grandkids can hold pictures they've drawn up to the camera, or your daughter can take the camera to scan the room to show you the new living room set.

Meetings. Also using the technology of videophony are meeting sites such as Zoom and Google Meet. Multiple people can meet simultaneously, each displayed on the screen and able to talk with each other. Usually a host sets up the meeting and sends a link to the other participants.

Popular apps. Currently popular gathering places on the web include facebook.com, twitter.com, and Instagram.com. On Facebook you have friends; on Twitter you have followers. When you sign on, you see the posts of your friends. You can reply or "like," and you can submit posts of your own to see if your friends reply.

When I go on Facebook, I feel nourished by the contact with people I know and care about. I don't feel as lonely afterwards. I "like" some posts just to show I am still around.

On opening my newslist, I find multiple posts just from the day before. One of my daughters-in-law posts pictures of my grandkids. Friends post what is new in their lives. Some of the other posts from friends are not personal but a pithy comment on life displayed in large type with colored background.

According to Pew Research Center, 44% of Americans got their news from Facebook in 2018.

Instagram. Instagram is similar to Facebook but you post and receive photos and short video clips. Usually you take the photos with your phone and post from there. Instagram has photo editing tools to make your pictures sharper, brighter, and eliminate background clutter.

Conclusion. The internet tools for messaging provide a surrogate for face-to-face encounters. They can be addictive. Decide how much of your time you want to spend on messaging, and then enjoy the rest of your day in other pursuits.

Challenge for Change. Get phone numbers from three new people the next time you see them. Have paper and pen handy, and offer to give them yours.

21. Deception

A Wolf found great difficulty in getting at the sheep owing to the vigilance of the shepherd and his dogs. But one day it found the skin of a sheep that had been flayed and thrown aside, so it put it on over its own pelt and strolled   down   among   the   sheep. The Lamb that belonged to the sheep, whose skin the Wolf was wearing, began to follow the Wolf in the Sheep's clothing; so, leading the Lamb a little apart, he soon made a meal off her, and for some time he succeeded in deceiving the sheep, and enjoying hearty meals. Appearances are deceptive.

Joseph Jacobs, *The Fables of Aesop*, London: Macmillan & Co., 1894.

Money. Two basic principles prevail:

1. You need money to live on. You may be getting by on Social Security or a Medicaid subsidy, or you may have assets of a stock portfolio and jewelry and real estate.

2. However much or little you have, some people would try to take your money. They are frequently called scammers or frauds. I call them thieves.

Although telemarketers, telephone solicitors, and certain trades people steal from elderly, the thieves can also include trusted professionals, caregivers, "sweethearts," and even family members.

Thieves will use tried-and-true scams to try to get you to hand over whatever is a significant sum of money to you. If you have $500, they'll try to part you from $100. If you have $50,000, they'll try for $10,000.

Elderly are particularly targeted because they are often isolated. It happens that a spouse dies and leaves behind a person unaccustomed to handling their own finances. Some amount of confusion might be present, but even the most mentally alert have been known to fall for scams.

An estimated 5 million cases of elder financial abuse occur in the United States each year. Only 1 in 25 cases are brought to the attention of law officials because of confusion or embarrassment.

Fraud report. If you suspect you have been a victim of a fraud, contact local authorities such as police and give them as much information as you can about it

Go to the web page for the National Center on Elder Abuse www.ncea.acl.gov for information on types of fraud and how to report. You can call their Elder Locator 800-677-1116 weekdays from 9 am to 8 pm ET for a referral to a local agency which will address your problem.

Also AARP has a Fraud Watch Network 877-908-3360 staffed by volunteers who take complaints concerning fraud.

Financial advisers. Maybe you handle your financial assets yourself, or maybe you let them be. If you want assistance in this area, you may want a financial adviser to help you sort through the array of investment opportunities, for example, stocks, bonds, mutual funds, precious metals, real estate, annuities.

A stock broker will build a portfolio for you, but she is working for herself. She gets paid when she makes a commission on buying and selling, and she benefits from advising you to buy and sell even if it doesn't make a great change in your position. When done to excess, it is called churning, a form of financial fraud. If she works for a well-known brokerage firm, she *may* have some degree of integrity.

A certified financial planner is a fiduciary, which means that he is committed to putting your best interests first. He may work based on a percentage of your assets or on an hourly rate. Clarify how he will be billing you, and ask to see his certificate.

Other professional designations include registered investment adviser (RIA), certified public accountant (CPA), and chartered financial analyst (CFA) as well as many more. You want someone who is competent and honest. Ask if they are part of a licensing organization, and check their credentials online.

Anyone can hang out a shingle and claim to be a financial adviser. No restriction is placed on who may use that term. Some don't even bother with the shingle but work from the phone, meet at your place, and disappear once they have taken what they can get, all with an endearing smile.

The bank has financial advisers as well, but they often promote specific products of the bank. What about a Client-Based Investment Contractor (CBIC)? Actually I just made that up, but it looks good. I could get a certificate printed up and frame it.

Check web sites. Google the name of the certifying or registering organization to see if they have data on their members, including experience and complaints.

A financial adviser should offer a wide variety of products and services. If he is only pushing one product or type of product, he may have a vested interest. Some advisers are also insurance salesmen who receive commissions.

Make sure that every financial transaction is cleared with you first. Keep a steno pad of the results of

your conversations. Get statements from the financial institution holding your money, and have statements sent to
a trusted but non-involved family member or friend as
well.

Take your time in making financial decisions. Give
yourself twenty-four hours to think it over. You don't
want a deal so volatile that it will change drastically in
that time. Do a little research. Who or what is behind this
offering? How solid are they?

11% of American investors personally lost money
because of fraud in a year. In other words, the scheme
worked.

Older people can call the Financial Industry Regu-
lating Hotline (FINRA) at 844-57-HELPS (844-574-
3577) with questions about brokerage accounts including
statements and individual investments. They accept calls
weekdays   9   am   to   5   pm   ET.   Also   see
www.brokercheck.finra.org to check on individual financial advisers who are registered. FINRA has been author-
ized by Congress to protect American investors.

Sweetheart scam. Suddenly a new person has entered your life, or a previous contact has shown a renewed interest. Perhaps you have contacted someone
over the internet who follows up with you. You hit it off
well. Fascinating, charming, and attentive, this person
represents what has been missing in your life. You meet
or correspond.

Don't discuss your assets with anyone except those
helping you with your finances. Don't indicate whether
you are comfortable or strapped for cash. Let the state of
your finances be an unknown.

He tells you he loves you. Three very powerful
words. Even though you are a cautious person, those
words sweep you off your feet. The incredible feeling

that someone loves you, yes loves you, brings a strong emotional response. You would do anything for this person.

The sweetheart has a problem. His sister needs surgery. His house needs a new roof. Whatever the problem, he asks for a significant loan. You feel hesitant, but you love him so much and he would never hurt you. Wanting to do what you can to show your love, you are tempted to write a check or get a cashier's check. *Just say no.*

Or he suggests—persists—that you take an investment opportunity, under the table but very lucrative, which he will arrange for you. *Just say no.*

It will be easier to say no if you have been paying your own way, if you have insisted on separate checks at dinner and bought your own movie tickets and popcorn. If you have been letting him wine and dine you, then you are more likely to have been entranced by the relationship and to feel beholden to him.

Thrill to the feeling of being in love, enjoy his company, but he is asking the unthinkable. Would you agree if he insisted that the two of you walk naked through the mall? Some things are not on the table of possibility. It is not right to ask the elderly for money, regardless of their financial status.

If you want to do what you can to prove your love, knit a sweater or bake a pie.

If he is genuine, he will stay. If he didn't have money for a new roof before he met you, he still doesn't have the money for a new roof but he does have the pleasure of your company.

Otherwise he may take off once he has the money, or he may stick around to see if he can get more with another story. At some point it ends, and you have been bilked out of tens of thousands of dollars. His phone number has been changed. You are emotionally hurt and embarrassed. You don't report it, don't even tell the kids, but keep hiding this sore spot in your heart.

I have used the masculine pronoun for the thief and the feminine for the victim, but of course it works the other way around. It may be someone the same age, older, younger. One cannot clearly see the wolf in sheep's clothing. The FTC reported that people over 60 lost $56 million in sweetheart scams in 2018.

Family. Unconscionable as it may seem, family members have been known to drain mom's assets. Motivated by greed, they figure they will inherit it eventually, and they may as well help themselves. Other family members have good intentions to manage mom's assets for her, but they "borrow" from the account for a vacation or a new car. Adopt some preventive strategies:

o Don't sign over control of all of your funds. If your family is helping to keep your monthly bills and expenses straight, give them access to your checking account only. If a withdrawal from savings is needed to cover the month's expenses, you withdraw just that amount and transfer it to checking. Keep the bulk of your assets under your control.

o Obtain and review all monthly statements. Be on the alert for unexplained withdrawals. Ask questions. Ask for receipts for withdrawals over a certain amount.

o Have a trusted friend or other relative receive and review all bank statements.

o If your grocery bill seems high, ask for the receipt from the grocery store. Make sure you are paying for only your own groceries.

o Ask your bank if they look for any red flags on senior accounts to help detect fraudulent activity, such as sudden large withdrawals or frequent maxing out at the ATM. Ask if they generate Suspicious Activity Reports.

o If your family wants a guardianship or conservatorship to take over your finances, they will have to get a court order. Hire a lawyer to represent you at the hearing.

If you truly can't manage your money and can't find anyone to do it, you can ask Social Security about a representative payee. Be forewarned that she will take control of your finances. She will decide how much to budget for grocery and how much for cable. She may even have the final say on whether you can withdraw from savings to make ends meet or whether you must live on an austerity budget.

Telephone scams. Never give out information over the phone, not your name or your grandkids' names or whether you rent or own or live in a facility and particularly not your identification numbers—Medicare, Social Security, driver's license or state ID, credit card numbers, birthdate. With this information thieves can apply for credit in your name, run up bills online, or steal your identity and create financial havoc that will take months to straighten out.

They can spoof a number on caller ID so that it looks like you are receiving a call from an agency like Social Security. De not give them any information including account numbers or date of birth. Hang up and call that agency directly. Some telephone numbers:

Medicare   800-633-4227 (800-MEDICARE)
Internal Revenue Service 800-829-0433
Social Security   800-772-1213

Also for Social Security, contact the Office of Inspector General 800-269-0271.

Medicare scam. Recently the government began issuing new Medicare cards. The numbers were no longer based on the Social Security Number but were a string of letters and numerals. Guard this number carefully. With this number someone can make fraudulent claims in your name or sell you cheap medical equipment at an inflated price.

A standard phone call from a Medicare thief may go something like this:

Thief: *Hello, Mr. Smith, this is Brenda Jones from Medicare. We have noticed some irregularities in your account that we need to straighten out.*

Victim: *What kind of irregularities?*

Thief: *I'm sure it's not a problem. The computer has flagged your account for cancellation, but with a little information from you we can rectify the situation. To verify who I'm talking to, please give me your Medicare account number.*

Victim: *I've heard you're not supposed to give your Medicare account number to anyone over the phone.*

Thief: *Where did you hear that?*

Victim: *I read it in a magazine for seniors.*

Thief: *Surely you don't believe everything you read. They just write those scare stories to increase their circulation. Fake news. How could we do business if we didn't use the phone? Your case requires immediate attention or the computer will shut you down.*

Victim: *I'm not sure.*

Thief: *It's your choice. But if the computer bumps you off the system, you will have to reapply. That could take months, and in that time you will be uninsured.*

Victim: *How do I know you're from Medicare? If you're from Medicare, you should know my number.*

Thief: *You're being unnecessarily difficult when I am trying to prevent problems. Of course I have your number, but I need for you to read it to me to verify it so that we can straighten your account. It's up to you.*

Victim: *All right. Let me get my card.*

Notice that the victim puts up a valiant struggle, but the thief beats him down. She engages his trust, but at the same time she ridicules him to break down his defenses. She stresses the urgency of the situation, not giving the victim time to think things through. Even though the victim has been warned of such a scheme, he reasons that giving the thief the identity number cannot do much harm. He is led to believe that the thief speaks with authority.

If someone calls claiming to be from Medicare, do not give her the opportunity to work on your fears. Hang up and call Medicare directly. Tell them about the phone call and ask if there is a problem with your account.

Family scams. A stranger calls and tells you:

o Your granddaughter has been kidnapped. You hear screams in the background. You must come up with money immediately.

o Your sister needs emergency surgery. The hospital won't admit her unless she pays some of her outstanding bill.

o Your nephew has been arrested in a foreign country. He needs bail money in order to be released.

You will be told to stay on the line. As hard as it is to do, hang up and contact your family immediately. If there is a crisis (there never is), they will know how you can help. Otherwise they will reassure you and put the granddaughter on the line.

Something for nothing scam. Unfortunately the way this works is that you put up something and receive nothing in return.

People "find" a wallet with money and offer to split it with you if you put up money to show your good faith.

Someone (often a foreign prince but it could be anybody) has inherited money but needs someone to put up some money to resolve some legal difficulties first. They will give you a generous portion of the inheritance in return.

Someone has received a consignment of expensive televisions and is willing to sell you one at under market value. When you open the box, you find a well-padded rock.

You have won the lottery, but you have to wire money for fees and taxes.

The stories and their variations go on forever. Essentially the story goes:

o You will receive a windfall of dubious origin.
o All you have to do is put up some money first.

Other. According to CNBC, one in eighteen older "cognitively intact" adults falls prey to financial fraud or abuse in a given year.

Money is solicited for fake charities, or even using the name of real charities but diverted to another recipient.

Pop-up browser windows offer fake software or even viruses.

Thieves call and tell you that they need to check your computer because it is creating a disturbance. They instruct you to enter certain keys which enable them to take over your computer.

A contractor "just happens" to be in your area and will fix the roof, seal the driveway, or do some other chore that he has noticed needs being done. Never pay in full up front. He will do half (or less) of the job for twice the price. He may use black paint on the roof to make it look repaired. If you need work done, find work persons through normal channels (neighbors, internet), and you contact them. Get more than one bid.

Review. We have presented a lot of information. A brief summary follows of red flags and ways to handle them.

Do not respond to unsolicited phone calls, emails, or personal contact at the door. If they say they are representing an agency, check with the agency. Exception: little girls in a Girl Scout uniform with a genuine cookie order form.

Do not give out information to someone you don't know. If it's the bank, call back at the number on your account statement.

Do not talk to someone you don't know. Hang up. Don't give them the opportunity to argue and beat you down.

Even if you do know someone, don't give them information about your financial status or where you keep your assets. Exceptions of course are those who are helping to handle your assets.

Do talk about your contacts, whom you're seeing socially, promises from brokers, etc, with family and friends. They may notice if something doesn't seem right. Remember that the wolf was successful because he separated the little lamb from the fold.

Check credentials/registration of financial advisers.

Double up on scrutiny. In addition to yourself, have a disinterested friend or family member review all statements, accounts, and reports from all sources including family.

Caller ID can be spoofed to show a different caller.

Do not believe a stranger who tells you of a family emergency. Check with family.

Do not believe that you can get something for nothing. You will get nothing.

Do not give to a charity over the phone unless you have called them at a published number (internet, television, publication).

Disregard pop-up windows, especially if they are telling you to restart your browser.

Never enter commands into your computer that someone on the phone suggests unless you have called them (a computer store, for instance).

Challenge for Change. It has all been so gloomy and a little bit frightening. You need a reprieve. Call someone just to chat, or be kind to yourself in some small way. Be not afraid.

22. Depression and Anxiety

Loneliness reflects how you feel about your relationships. Depression reflects how you feel, period.
John T. Cacioppoa and William Patrick, *Loneliness.*

Lack of social contact and poor physical health can cause depression in an older person. It may go undetected because people expect these changes in the elderly. If diagnosed, it can be treated with positive outcomes.

While feelings of loneliness may contribute to depression, the depression can cause social withdrawal and further isolation. Thus the two form a downward spiral, each feeding off of the other. With help you can break out of this, and you move in a more positive direction.

Symptoms of major depressive disorder. Consider a six-cylinder car running on four (or fewer) cylinders. The car goes, but progress is balky, uneven, and slow. This image helps explain some of the symptoms of major depressive disorder. Depressed brains run slowly. The symptoms reflect that. You may have several of these symptoms but not necessarily all of them:

o **Fatigue.** If your engine stutters and sputters, you find it harder to do the ordinary. You may not be able to keep up with the day. Understandably you feel less energetic.

o **Lack of interest in anything.** Decreased interest in pleasure. Remember that you are not receiving full sensory input. Some of the impulses short-circuit. As a result things you might once have enjoyed seem far away, pale. A tree that might have once seemed majestic is now just a stick with leaves on it. You look past it. A recipe you might have once been eager to try now just fights your fatigue in an unending series of steps.

o **Anxiety.** I discuss this in more depth later. You look okay to everyone else. You are running an obstacle course with shackles around your ankles. At any moment you might be required to do something beyond your endurance. You are apprehensive about the present, about the future.

o **Difficulty concentrating.** You find it difficult to pay attention. Words slide over you. They are not input. If you have a mental task, it just lies there before you like a box with a lock. You can't get into it. In adding a column of numbers, you can't remember what to carry.

o **Feelings of worthlessness or guilt.** You are comparing yourself to the way you used to be, or perhaps you are comparing yourself to others. That's not fair. You can't compare four cylinders to six. Leave off comparing. Live in the moment. This is you. If you are surviving the moment, however brutally, this suffices.

o **Blues or low mood.** You no longer experience joy or pleasure in ordinary events. All of this adds up to feeling permanently down.

o **Disturbances in eating or sleeping.** You may miss meals as too much effort. You may snack between meals as self-consolation. You may have difficulty falling asleep, even more difficulty staying asleep. Your fatigued body is having trouble getting signals from the rhythms of the day. You fall asleep in the daytime. You have trouble adhering to your circadian rhythms.

o **Recurrent thoughts of death.** As the depression deepens, as the difficulty in functioning in ordinary ways becomes greater, as the feelings of self-worth slide, you may reach the point where it doesn't seem possible to keep going. The fact is that at this point it isn't possible to keep going, but nobody notices the depth of your struggles.

Depression screening. If you Google "depression screening," you will find several options for a brief multiple choice test which will give you an indication of level of depression if any. I scored "mildly depressed," which surprised me since I feel good. I suppose that after several times in my life when I battled more severe depression, a state of mildly depressed would feel good.

Personal experience. My first severe depression occurred in my early thirties. I retreated to the chair and couldn't make myself do anything. Hour after hour went by when I was telling myself that I must mop the kitchen floor, that I had skipped it the previous week and the week before that.

My mind went off on adventures of its own and I started to think of other things. What things I never knew. When I came out of it, I couldn't remember what I had been thinking about. I couldn't concentrate. I hurt but never could point to what hurt.

Over the next several years I saw psychiatrists and took medications. I believe frequent meetings of support groups or day programs with people with similar problems helped most. Faith played a key role.

My head returned to functioning, and I was able to concentrate to some level again. I worked for twenty years for the county board as an advocate for people with mental illness until I retired. The job further completed my healing, but it had to come at a time when I was ready for it.

Brain function. What had changed to make living so difficult? Some say a change in the brain chemistry makes the difference. In the brain, messages are transmitted by brain cells known as neurons (200 billion in the brain alone). Messages between neurons process sensory input, cognitive function, and other. Between each neuron is a gap called a synapse. The impulse cannot cross this gap unless a chemical called a neurotransmitter is present. In depression the neurotransmitter is often lacking to some extent so that messages cannot traverse the brain as well. Thus a physiological difference in the brain causes the symptoms of depression.

A doctor who prescribes medication to boost the chemical levels of the brain usually treats.major depressive disorder. Often psychotherapy is also indicated as the patient's mood and activities can play key roles in recovery.

Push/pull. I was always faced with the question of whether to push forward or pull back in my activities. I felt burned out, and everything seemed an effort. I was tempted to lay low until it passed, isolate, not take on anything. Yet to leave the brain swimming in its chemistry of negative thoughts meant to stay in the depression.

Push forward or pull back? I found the answer is yes to both. Get out there and do something, contact someone, see something new, take out a library book, stop at Starbucks. It doesn't have to be a huge event, just enough to get the neurons popping. Times Square on New Year's Eve might be a bit much at first.

Schedule quiet times between your activities to allow your brain to feel the afterglow quietly. Reflect positively on where you've been and what you've done. Even if it is raining buckets, the event registers as a different experience from staying home. Consider yourself as building strength like a weightlifter, hoisting barbells for a number of reps and then resting the muscle to give it a chance to build up.

As noted, one of the key symptoms of depression is "don't wanna, not gonna." Unable to motivate oneself to do anything, a person prefers to be left alone in their depression. In this sense the depression is seductive. One wants to snuggle up against it and stay there. Leave me alone. And yet one experiences pain.

Just as stress to a muscle can cause injury and pain, so too mental stress, grieving, and fatigue can cause the brain chemistry to change. On occasion no apparent trigger manifests itself. Genetic predisposition plays a role. I can point to my family tree.

A reversal of this negative thought pattern can help bring one out of depression. A supportive environment rather than a blaming environment makes a difference. This goes especially for self-blaming. Accept your illness as illness.

One choice: to ask for help, insist on help. Seek out medical professionals who specialize in depression, especially psychiatrists. If they put you on meds, remember to take them.

Another choice is to stop trying, to retreat from the world as much as possible. I know more than one person who has simply taken to bed for years at a time.

Suicide. And the last, and worst, choice is to end your life. Another way out can always be found, even when people aren't listening to your cries for help. If you are already getting help, give it a chance to work or try someplace else.

In my experience, suicidal ideation is addictive. One consoles oneself with the idea that it will all be over. This sets off a relief response in the brain. One returns to the thoughts to get more of this consolation, setting up an addictive cycle. The thoughts become real.

After years of playing this game, I have found it best not to entertain the thoughts. At first I worried that if I suppressed the thoughts, they would secretly grow stronger in some underground river of my soul. I have found that not to be the case.

Call the national suicide hotline number at 800-273-8255. If you are being afflicted with thoughts of self-termination, bring those thoughts out into the open. Suicide is a bad idea. I care about you and want you to live. Let go of the thoughts. Get help. You will look back on it as "those days when…," but the point is you will be present to look back on it.

Anxiety. Like depression, anxiety can hit a person with varying levels of intensity. You are familiar with moments of anxiety that manifest themselves when you are faced with something new or stressful. The feelings resolve themselves once the hurdle has been overcome.

At the other extreme, chronic anxiety never seems to go away. It may manifest itself physically in the head, the gut, the shoulders, the back. Trembling may be present. It intensifies at times of stress. It may have its origins in real-life problems with job, money, relationships, but not necessarily.

Damage control. If applicable, assess the part of your body that is sending out distress signals. Treating with a pain reliever or stomach remedy may help you feel calmer.

Take a deep breath, hold it a couple of seconds, and let it out slowly. Do this a few more times. Of all stress reduction techniques, deep breathing comes most highly recommended.

Physically move. Take a walk, dance, do some exercises.

Make contact with someone.

Make something happen. Engage in an activity that you enjoy, like reading a book or building a model airplane. Or take care of a task that has been bugging you, like cleaning the refrigerator.

Set milestones. At the top of every hour, reflect how you made it through the previous hour and determine how you will make it through the next hour. I set my snooze on my alarm clock so that it goes off every hour.

Eat healthy meals with plenty of veggies and a helping of protein. Give your body something to work with. If you hype it up with sudden bursts of sugar, you will pay in the long run.

Similarly watch your caffeine intake including sodas. Even if you are feeling down, don't allow yourself more than you are used to, maybe even less. I keep bottles of flavored water on hand.

Stress analysis. Identify your anxiety. It may be an upcoming social event, like Thanksgiving dinner at your house with twenty-two family members.

One year with a smaller crowd I made out a minute-by-minute itinerary of the last two hours of prep time: when to peel the potatoes, start the green beans, take the turkey out, make the gravy, mash the potatoes. I've never since done it to that detail, but for that one year it was what I needed. Take the potatoes off the stove at 3:47 and drain them.

You can't control the twenty-two guests. If Uncle Hank and Uncle George argued politics last year, odds are that they will argue politics this year. It's not your problem. If they become too loud, the other guests will try to neutralize them.

Another scenario could be that you are dreading an upcoming social situation, say an afternoon barbecue at the residence. You fear you will be embarrassed by not being able to come up with a comment. Margaret snags you and tries to talk to you about the new social director who is clearly incompetent. Have prepared some innocuous comments which will fit in for whatever complaint someone brings up.

I hadn't noticed that.
I'm surprised to hear that.
That's very interesting.
It's supposed to rain tomorrow.

In this life, if you are prepared to handle a complaint, you are prepared for most conversations.

Some people can be anxious about being anxious. I have a friend Millie for whom family gatherings cause a lot of anxiety. She fears that she would become noticeably agitated at the event and ruin it for everyone. It had happened before when she hadn't anticipated it, and it had blindsided her.

After acknowledging this fear, Millie is better able to monitor herself at events and retreat if she needs a few moments to get hold of herself. Also she has discussed the situation with her closest family members who were able to be supportive. They assured her that the previous event had not seemed nearly as huge to anyone else as it had to her, and it had not ruined it for anyone else even though it felt that way.

Cycle. Anxiety can wear down the brain and increase depression, while depression can slow response time and feed anxiety. The two must be tackled simultaneously. Professional help often increases positive effects.

- o *Push forward.* Make small commitments to contact people either in your room in a skilled nursing facility or if you have the ability to go out.
- o *Look forward.* Analyze what may be expected of you. Prepare yourself.
- o *Fall back.* After the event, allow yourself to rest, read a book, or watch television. Reflect on your outing. Find what was good about it. Reflect if you learned anything to make it easier next time.

Addiction. Another bad choice. More and more of a substance does less and less for you. Where one benzo (valium, xanax, ativan, etc.) a day used to ease the pain, now it takes two. After a while you need three, but the doctor won't prescribe that many. You take three anyhow and run out early. You call the doctor in tears and tell him you left them on the bus. Or you ask around until you can find street drugs. You are hooked. It works the same with pain pills like oxycontin.

You may turn to alcohol. Where one drink used to do, now it takes two and three and more to achieve the same effect. You go through the day partly inebriated. It disturbs your sleep. Your grandkids don't want hugs.

Baby boomers are particularly known to be casual with drugs. DrugRehab.com reports that there are 2.5 million older adults with an alcohol or drug problem. If you are already addicted, seek treatment specifically for older adults. Because of differences in metabolism, during withdrawal you can experience a higher seizure risk, heart arrhythmia, or higher blood pressure. Trained staff can manage these outcomes.

Doctors no longer prescribe benzos or pain killers so liberally. If you are in pain, physical or psychological, ask for therapies and other methods to treat your pain.

If you are currently not leaning on a substance of abuse, resist the temptation to start. You can't run away from depression on a subterfuge of substance. You will wind up with two problems where you had only one.

Getting help. Don't stop to consider whether you need help. The question is do you want help? Would you like the feeling of having someone in your court? You may not need a hand weeding the big vegetable garden, but help sure is nice to have.

A psychiatrist is a medical doctor (M.D.) trained in mental health including depression and anxiety. Like other medical doctors, they can write prescriptions. Often a psychiatrist does mostly medication management with brief appointments at sporadic intervals. A few still do psychotherapy. Some work in an office in conjunction with a therapist.

Practitioners of therapy come with a wide variety of labels: psychologist (often with a degree of Psy.D.), counselor, therapist, social worker (usually L.I.S.W.), and a wide variety of self-proclaimed labels such as life contingency analyst or yoga therapist. Check both the degree they hold (a must) and experience.

Philosophies differ. If you find you don't like the approach of one therapist, try another. Some strictly listen while others engage with you more. After a couple of sessions, decide if you are comfortable with this person.

Try your local Area Agency on Aging (see www.n4a.org) for recommendations. You can also look up practicing therapists in Psychology Today (www.psychologytoday.com/us/therapists). For a psychiatrist, ask a local hospital with a psychiatric unit for the name of someone who practices there and is taking outside patients. Also ask about outpatient support groups.

Challenge for Change. Execute a push-forward action. Come home and make notes.

23. A Cure for Loneliness

Grow old along with me!
The best is yet to be,
The last of life, for which the first was made:
Robert Browning, "Grow Old Along With Me,"
Immortal Poems of the English Language

Celebration. Come celebrate with me. We have been on a journey together. We started by acknowledging our feelings of loneliness and the need for change.

In the process, you looked at how you see yourself so that you could spot the self-doubts. You refuted your negative inner critic and affirmed to yourself. You are more at peace internally and have begun to approach others with confidence. Possibly you are already making friends. If not, you will.

The battle. The combat against loneliness can be broken into two phases:

1. Solitude—comfortable when alone, or
2. Companionship—more in contact with people.

Both require some effort on your part, but I have detailed the steps in the previous chapters.

Solitude. Being alone does not necessarily imply loneliness. Solitude means being comfortable while alone as in Chapter 5. You have learned to meditate in chapter 6, to control your breathing and dispel unwanted thoughts.

Choose to spend more time just being alone with your thoughts. Maybe you look out the window or sip iced tea while you contemplate life. Even if your thoughts are negative, you can put a positive spin on them by practicing forgiveness and charity.

Amuse yourself during times of solitude by being active. Chapters 7-9 are brimming with activities to do at home, places to go, or opportunities for volunteering or employment.

You can look at your particular lifestyle to find opportunities for people contact, whether it is independent living, assisted living, or skilled nursing facility.

Conversation. Being able to express yourself to another and to receive confirmation from that person plays such an important role in whether you will be able to overcome loneliness. A person presents himself as an outside shell until you learn more about what is inside him. You become acquaintances.

You can accept a wide variety of persons to be your social acquaintances, but you want your friends to be compatible. How do you establish compatibility?

When two dogs meet, they sniff, they bark, they circle around each other. They use nonverbal cues to establish if they are friendly or hostile. They can't ask each other if they have grandkids.

While we as humans do our share of nonverbal circling around, we have the gift of language that we can use to find out about each other and establish compatibility. In order to initiate friendships, use this gift to get to know people. When you encounter someone, give to them from the warmth of your person. Embark on a mutual journey. If you remain within yourself, you will know only yourself, and you will be lonely.

Friendship. You are ready for friendship, a special reciprocal relationship. You trust this person to accept you, to allow you to initiate contact to overcome your loneliness, and even to welcome your contact. Likewise you are there for your friend.

As part of the cure, you have to work at friend-ships. If someone texts you, then follow through. Initiate contact with people and overcome their inhibitions. Be willing to give and even to love. To overcome loneliness, invest a piece of yourself.

Four-letter words. Some four-letter words sum-marize the process:

- cure
- work
- self
- talk
- gift
- love

Cure. The system works. I have thought through the ramifications of loneliness and researched it and re-lated topics. I have followed my own advice, and it has paid off. My life feels fuller. I have some people I call friends. I feel more connected.

I have my writing group and the senior center. My neighbor and I chat in the hall. I strike up more conversa-tions with strangers with whom I share time and space. Even though fleeting, these encounters enrich my day.

If I want company, I have people I can call. Occa-sionally I meet with friends at a fast food. I am closer to my siblings. I email and phone. The transition happened over a period of time, but the cure works. You can make it work for you as well.

Work. If you always flow downstream adhering to your old habits, then you will be lonely. You have to re-sist the temptation to stay quietly and safely in the corner. At the idea of speaking up, your inhibitions cut in, and you have to push them aside like paddling against the current.

Once you have friendships, work with them so that they do not become cool from lack of attention. You can so easily let the afternoon slip by without reaching out to anyone. Pretty soon you are not on anybody's radar, and you have to start over catching up to people.

Work to make your times of solitude meaningful. If you plan to knit, you will arrange to have yarn on hand, either purchased at a store or ordered online or procured by a friend or caregiver. However you plan to spend your time of solitude, prepare for it so that it won't be lonely. Do you have a deck of cards, a jigsaw puzzle, a book? Somewhere to go?

Self. Inner voices that are decades old try to tear you down. The negative voices speak more strongly than the positive ones only to the extent that you believe them, that you let them have the last word. Where does this trash-talk come from—an employer, a parent, a lover?

This self-criticism doesn't arise from your inner person. You need to tell these voices of memories from others to quite literally shut up so that you can listen to the real you. Find the good in yourself and believe it.

Approach other people with confidence. Do a quick mental check and tell yourself that you are up to this. Smile.

You are unique. You have something to offer. I imagine I am the only person in my apartment building who simultaneously roots for both the Reds and the Dodgers, who has two kids living in Ohio and one in California, and who writes. As topics of conversation, I can talk about the property manager, about baseball, about the problems of relating to grown kids, about a writing group.

Take care of yourself—nutrition, sleep, exercise. Use your times of solitude in ways that give back to you. Believe in yourself.

Talk. One tradition has it that on the first day of every month, the first words out of your mouth should be "rabbits, rabbits, rabbits." If you remember, you will receive lots of presents during the month.

My daughter tries, but she is often distracted by her husband or kids before she remembers. I usually get it, unless I talk to myself as I occasionally do. I have no one else to talk to. In order to keep the conversational part of me alive, I have to make up my mind to seek out encounters, whether with strangers on the van or by email or phone with friends.

Where people are gathered, follow up on your reason for being there.

Do you come to bingo every week?

Is this your first tenant meeting?

Note mutual acquaintances you spot in the room Move on to more general topics, like the inflated price of a loaf of bread.

With friends, you can let the conversation flow in whatever direction it chooses. Remember the guidelines for good conversation. Reciprocate. Empathize. Give and get information on how you are and how you want to be. It takes effort to pay attention to a conversation and to be there for another.

Loneliness isolates people. Communication connects people. In order to overcome loneliness, you have to be willing to open your mouth and talk.

Gift. In talking reveal yourself; make a gift of yourself. If you paid for someone's dinner but sat silently through the meal, you haven't given to him. You may play a game of cards with someone, but if you haven't said a word, you haven't made a gift of yourself to her.

Be gracious. Put aside your aching back and affirm the dental assistant's hair-do. Hold a door, let someone in line, write a note, do a random act of kindness.

Give to your friends. Find the energy to be enthusiastic. Reach into your feelings and sincerely care about their concerns. Assist when feasible. Give to them part of yourself, how you feel, what you have been doing or thinking. Trust them with the best part of your being.

Does your friend have a need? Perhaps someone to help her with her mail, or to hold the skein of yarn while she winds it into a ball. Do you have a need? Perhaps someone to go with you to look for a present for your daughter-in-law. These moments of giving make the memories of a friendship.

Love. Make the choice to feel love for all that is around you. Love yourself. Love your neighbor. Love your enemy. What of the physical therapist who barks orders at me and in general makes my life miserable? I can resolve to treat him civilly if not with detached amusement. I can try not to make his day more difficult than it already is; indeed I can try to add something to his day.

Love the day. Love the oatmeal and the cloud shaped like a teddy bear and the breeze. Love the delivery guy and the woman on the radio. Sway to the music. Love your body. Love coffee with a friend or a solitary walk. You can love it all if you choose to.

Tools. By now you have the tools to combat loneliness. If you have just been reading along in the book but haven't implemented any of the suggested changes, go back and review the improvements offered. Start by loving yourself so that you are comfortable in solitude. Reach out to others. Come celebrate them with me.

Challenge for Change. The Challenges for Change are listed in the back. Review them and pick one to implement today. Repeat tomorrow.

24. The Ultimate Friend

All men have access to God, but each man has a different access. Mankind's great chance lies precisely in the unlikeness of men, in the unlikeness of their qualities and inclinations. God's all-inclusiveness manifests itself in the infinite multiplicity of the ways that lead to him, each of which is open to one man.

Martin Buber, "The Way of Man According to the Teachings of Hasidism"

The passenger. I can discuss the topics related to the cure for loneliness without reference to God, and I have so far for the sake of those of you who would reject a book on spirituality. But now in this final chapter, which you can skip if you choose, I bring God into the concept of battling loneliness.

God is the Ultimate Friend. Always present, God will insure that you are never all alone. You will always have your God to call on.

You may also need human warmth, but God accompanies you on that search. It is as if you had run out of gas on the highway. You have a passenger to accompany you on that isolated walk to the nearest gas station, or even a friendly motorist to pick you up and give you a ride. You are in a predicament, but you are not alone.

God moments. At the senior center, round tables with six chairs each are spread out over the ballroom-sized room. Someone threading through the maze places her hand on my back as she passes by, a simple gesture of recognition and friendship. God is like that simple presence. God touches me to say "I am here" when I am caught up in trying to get through the day.

One day I walked into the library to pick up a couple of novels. Seated in an alcove was my friend Frances. That encounter with someone I knew in itself counts as a gift from God in the midst of the day.

Frances told me that she had found a wonderful book and held up the most recent copy of *Writer's Market*, the very tool I needed to start my own search into publishing. The library had a reference copy.

I felt God was telling me to get serious about writing a query and seeking an agent, a scary but necessary step. What if the book was no good? What if nobody wanted it? God was not making promises but telling me to try. I will do that. If you are reading this book, you know how it turned out.

As Buber said above, God has many means of access. Like a disco ball with multiple facets, God reflects light to each one of us in a distinct way. I share with you who God is for me, knowing we are all unique. By whatever name we call God, or if we do not call on God at all, we are all bathed in the same light each from his own mirrored source.

Friend. I believe God is present to us. At the risk of anthropomorphizing God, I can experience God and treat God as a friend.

When I am still, at times I feel God's presence. By simple affirmation I can know God is there. I may still feel lonely for human companionship, but I am not alone. I treat God as a friend. I talk to God. I present God with the quandaries of human relationships. What's up with that, Lord? I tell God of my aches and pains, and it feels good to know I have been heard.

Supreme Being. Before I get too cozy, I recognize also God as Supreme Being. God creates and sustains. God is love, but that means more than a fuzzy feeling. Love is God's commandment.

God expects me to live that law of love. When faced with a decision, I have to ask what love would have me do. When I violate that law, either by making a catty remark or by holding up a bank at gunpoint, the smoothness of our relationship is disrupted. When I recognize my folly and turn back to God, I am taken in. Although still a friend, God has expectations.

Source. All love comes from God because that's what God is. When I greet someone on the elevator, the love which impels me to do so comes from God within. When I forgive someone for standing me up, the ability to truly let go comes from God.

Sameness. According to St. Thomas Aquinas, God neither angers nor is sorrowful but is always unchanging. The filter of our imperfect being, in relationship to a fickle world, makes the difference in our perception of God. At times we say that God smiles, while at others we say that God frowns, depending on our circumstances of the moment. In fact God is not a Cheshire cat with a vanishing smile. God is constant. Our discernment of God changes.

God's answer. I am only one person in my own relationship with God, but if I were to ask the God I know to speak up for the divine point of view, I feel the dialogue would be something like this.

Me: What do you have to say for yourself, Almighty God? I am giving you an entire chapter to explain yourself. You say you created us to love, and yet some of us go through the day, go through entire days, without finding someone to love. Are we nor looking in the right places? Is it all our own fault?

God: I want to say something everyone will believe, in which everyone will find hope, but not everyone is open to those words. People are not able to hear them. They do not understand that my plan is that they should struggle with the weeds sown in the field by those who do not love.

So many words to describe me, and not one word that characterizes me. I am infinite, omnipotent, omniscient, eternal creator God. I am rock and shepherd and tree of life. Most importantly, I am.

I am Yahweh and Christ and Allah and Buddha and Brahma. I ask that my people love and do good. Some are inclined to attend to me and my truths, to pray and to contemplate.

I know that your world is not perfect, that it inflicts sorrows on you. One tradition has it that the world was perfect until that bite out of the apple. At times you bring down sorrow upon yourselves; at other times it is random like a tsunami. I am with you through it all.

Me: This is what I hear God saying in my heart. What does God say in yours?

Challenge for Change. Take a moment to tell God hello. What is in your heart to say to God?

Farewell

For many months now I have been writing to you, my reader. I didn't have a particular person in mind, other than that you are lonely and old, as are many people. As the book progressed, I envisioned your confidence growing. In my mind you became more outgoing and said "hello" readily. If this transformation has not completely taken place, don't give up. It's okay.

I have never met you, but I have come to love you dearly. You have been present to me when I was alone. Perhaps someday we will meet. If not, there are plenty of other people in the world to meet. Go find them.

karen mo
lonelygoldfish.net

Challenges for Change

Chapter 1. Smile. Whenever you think of it, smile to yourself. Let your lips turn up. You will feel better. Especially smile to other people when you encounter them, whether passing on a sidewalk or sitting down to dinner with them. Make it a habit to smile.

Chapter 2. Cold and Alone. How lonely are you? On the internet you can find a quiz which you can take to rate your degree of loneliness. If you Google "UCLA Loneliness Scale," you will find half a dozen websites which reprint this quiz.

Chapter 3. Born Lonely. Think of a friendly comment, perhaps for encountering a person in an elevator or in the grocery line. Examples:

It is {hot/cold/windy} today.

I like your {blouse/shoes/tie}.

Did you hear how the {Reds/Patriots/Lakers} did last night?

You can use these or come up with something better. Have your comment ready, and try it sometime.

Chapter 4. Self-Esteem. Capture a negative thought, a self put-down. You are never entirely free of them. Challenge it using the three steps outlined above. Lay the thought to rest. (If you are thinking, "I can't do this," then challenge that thought. Where does it come from? Who says you can't? Now do it.)

Chapter 5. Solitude. Make a loose schedule for today or tomorrow. Set mealtimes, bedtimes, and exercise times. If you have opportunities for social contact, in person or by phone, pencil them in. Arrange your solitary activities around these anchors.

Chapter 6. Meditation and Mindfulness. Try it.

Chapter 7. Activities at Home. Do an act of kindness for someone.

Chapter 8. Getting Out. Find a museum or dedicated site in your town that you had not known about.

Chapter 9. Volunteering and Part-Time Positions. Make a broad list of your skills, from child care to accounting to closet-organizing. Look for patterns and possible uses for these skills. If it's closet-organizing, then apply to a homeless shelter which receives clothing donations or a consignment shop.

Chapter 10. Downsizing. Live in the moment. What do you need to be doing right now? Anything else that needs to be done is not pertinent for now. Perhaps you need to be sorting bookshelves. On the other hand, perhaps you need to take an interesting book you came across and sit down with it without guilt. Live in the moment

Chapter 11. Independent Living. Especially if you live alone, sit somewhere different this evening, even if only for an hour. See the room from a new perspective.

Chapter 12. Institutional Living. If you live in an institutional setting, give it a homey touch—a plant, a picture on the wall or dresser, something created by your grandchild. Talk about it to people who come to your room.

Chapter 13. Dining Alone. Have something different for dinner, something you never had before, whether at home or out.

Chapter 14. Sleeping Alone. Think of one good thing that happened to you today. Save it for tonight if you need it.

Chapter 15. Sick and Alone. You have a job ahead of you. Make sure that you have all of the following information written down somewhere where you can get to it easily.

> Primary care physician: name, phone number, address.
> Other specialist(s): name, phone number, address.
> Someone who can help: Name, phone number.
> Urgent care: Name, phone number, address.
> Emergency room: Hospital, phone number.

Pharmacy: Name, phone number.
Alternate pharmacy (delivers): Name, phone number.
Ask-A-Nurse: phone number.
Cash or credit card for cab.
ID and insurance cards.

Also have a list of the medications you take, the dose, the frequency for the hospital.

Chapter 16. Community Efforts. Call your city government and ask what is being done for the socialization of the elderly.

Chapter 17. Conversation. Think of at least three topics you could use in a conversation.

Chapter 18. Friendship. Acknowledge someone. It can be a phone call to an old friend you haven't heard from recently or a shy "Hi" to a stranger in the elevator. Open the door.

Chapter 19. Making Friends. Draw concentric circles and map out the important people in your life. Look to see who you have been neglecting. How could you be loving them better? Pick up the phone.

Chapter 20. Telecommunication. Get phone numbers from three new people the next time you see them. Have paper and pen handy, and offer to give them yours.

Chapter 21. Deception. It has all been so gloomy and a little bit frightening. You need a reprieve. Call someone just to chat, or be kind to yourself in some small way. Be not afraid.

Chapter 23. A Cure for Loneliness. Review the Challenges for Change and pick one to implement today. Repeat tomorrow.

Chapter 24. The Ultimate Friend. Take a moment to tell God hello. What is in your heart to say to God?

References

American Psychological Association, "By the numbers: Older adults living alone," May 2016 vol. 47, no. 5.

Brown, Brenė, *Braving the Wilderness*, Random House, New York, 2017.

Cacioppoa, John T., and William Patrick, *Loneliness*, W. W. Norton & Company, Inc. New York, NY, 2008.

Carnegie, Dale, *How To Win Friends and Influence People*, Gallery Books, New York, NY, 1936.

Chödrön, Pema, *How To Meditate,* Sounds True, Inc., Boulder, CO, 2013.

Dienstmass, Giovanni, *Practical Meditation*, DK Publishing, New York, NY, 2018.

Dumm, Thomas, *Loneliness as a Way of Life*, Harvard University Press, Cambridge, MA, 2008.

Epstein, Joseph, *Friendship: An Exposé*, Houghton Mifflin Company, New York, NY, 2006.

Floyd, PhD,, Kory, *The Loneliness Cure*, Adams Media, Avon, MA, 2015.

Grayling, A.C., *Friendship*, Yale University Press, New Haven, CT, 2013.

Kaplan, Daniel, Barkman, Barbara, and Fitzdale, Ruth, "Older People Living Alone," Merck Manuals.

Kaufman, Walter, selected, *Religion from Tolstoy to Camus,* Harper & Row, New York, NY, 1961.

Leaver, Kate, *The Friendship Cure*, The Overlook Press, Peter Mayer Publishers, Inc. New York, NY, 2018.

Leland, John, *Happiness Is a Choice You Make, Lessons from a year among the oldest old*, Sarah Crichton Books, Farrar, Straus and Giraux, New York, NY, 2018.

Maitland, Sara, *How To Be Alone*, Picador, New York, NY, 2014.

McKay, Matthew, and Patrick Fanning, *Self-Esteem*, 3rd ed., New Harbinger Publications, Inc., Oakland, CA, 2000.

Mipham, Sakyong, *The Lost Art of Good Conversation*, Harmony Books, New York, NY, 2017.

Rohr, Richard, *Falling Upward, A Spirituality for the Two Halves of Life,* Jossey-Bass, San Francisco, CA, 2011.

Salzberg, Sharon, *Lovingkindness*, Shambala Publishers, Inc., Boulder, CO, 1995.

Teresa of Avila, St., *The Life of Teresa of Jesus*, E. Allison Peers, transl., Image Books, Garden City, NY, 1960.

Terrell, John Edward, *A Talent for Friendship*, Oxford University Press, New York, NY, 2015.

Made in the USA
Las Vegas, NV
13 July 2021